SpringerBriefs in Computer Science

Ricardo Couto Antunes da Rocha
Markus Endler

Context Management for Distributed and Dynamic Context-Aware Computing

 Springer

Ricardo Couto Antunes da Rocha
Institute of Informatics
Federal University of Goias (UFG)
Goiania-GO
Brazil

Markus Endler
Department of Informatics
Pontifícia Universidade Católica (PUC)
  do Rio de Janeiro
Rio de Janeiro-RJ
Brazil

ISSN 2191-5768   ISSN 2191-5776 (electronic)
ISBN 978-1-4471-4019-1   ISBN 978-1-4471-4020-7 (eBook)
DOI 10.1007/978-1-4471-4020-7
Springer London Heidelberg New York Dordrecht

Library of Congress Control Number: 2012936110

Printed on acid-free paper

Springer is part of Springer Science+Business Media (www.springer.com)

To my beloved wife, Renata
Ricardo

Acknowledgments

We would like to thank all members of the Laboratory for Advanced Collaboration (LAC), PUC-Rio, for the constant feedback to this work. In particular, we would like to thank Vagner, Hana, Fernando Ney, Antonio Theophilo, Gustavo, Marcelo Malcher, José Viterbo, Juliana e Bruno Silvestre.

We specially wish to thank Noemi de La Rocque Rodriguez (PUC-Rio), Renato Cerqueira (PUC-Rio), Antonio Alfredo Ferreira Loureiro (UFMG), and Artur Ziviani (LNCC). Their comments and critics help us to improve the quality of this book.

Contents

Chapter 1
Introduction

Abstract Research in context-aware computing has produced a number of application prototypes, frameworks, middleware systems and models for describing context. However, development of ubiquitous context-aware applications is still a difficult task because current middleware systems are focused on isolated and static context-aware environments. For example, applications require a global knowledge of the context-aware infrastructures in order to establish context-based interactions, and they suffer of problems such as disruptions when a context-aware environment evolves. This chapter introduces an approach for distributed context-aware computing that allows applications to maintain context-based continuous interactions, even in a dynamic environment. This chapter summarizes the limitations of current research in middleware for context-aware computing, as well the main contributions of this work.

Keywords Distributed context management · Context-aware computing · Middleware · Context evolution

1.1 Background

The goal of context-aware computing is to allow applications and services to perform adaptations at the occurrence of pre-defined context-based situations. Context information is data that describes the state of a certain entity at a specific moment [11]. For example, an application running on a portable device may change the rate of sending network messages if the battery level drops below 50%. In this case, the context information that triggers the adaptation is the percentage of remaining energy in the battery, which is the state of the device's power resources. This book adopts the term *context interest* to specify a context-based situation that triggers such an application-specific adaptation.

Modern operating systems for mobile devices, such as iPhone OS and Android, provide APIs to access embedded sensors, such as GPS, accelerometers, light

R. C. A. da Rocha and M. Endler, *Context Management for Distributed and Dynamic Context-Aware Computing*, SpringerBriefs in Computer Science, DOI: 10.1007/978-1-4471-4020-7_1, © The Author(s) 2012

sensors and power management system, which may act as context providers. However, complex context-aware applications require a more sophisticated mechanism to deal with context interest. For example, to obtain the list of devices currently located in a room, an application may need to contact location sensors at several devices in the room (e.g., a presence sensor). In such distributed scenarios, some sensors may be external to the device that maintains the context interest and may require an external computational infrastructure that stores and disseminate context. For example, a location sensor for indoor environments may be provided by an external service, such as in [29] and [23]. Middleware systems and frameworks should provide primitives that support transparency of sensor location and subscription of contextual situations and asynchronous notifications when a context situation satisfies an interest. The computational element responsible for binding context providers and applications is called *context management system* (CMS). A CMS is responsible for registering context interests and checking them against previously probed context information.

Research in context-aware computing has produced a number of frameworks [10, 20, 28], middleware systems [13, 14, 18, 24, 25, 31] and complex models [1, 5, 15] for describing and processing context. Their adoption, however, has been limited, in part because most solutions are restricted to specific applications, centralized architectures, limited physical domains or scopes. For example, the CoBrA infrastructure [4] provides mechanisms for context inference and models that are specific for smart meeting-room applications, such as described in [4].

In particular, most systems must be deployed and used in environments with predictable [22] behavior and characteristics, i.e. they cannot be deployed in distributed and dynamic scenarios because they are unable to deal with the idiosyncrasies of various environments, such as the diversity of sensors and context models. Middleware systems that address such requirements typically do not offer generality, flexibility or reuse.

T-Mobile's Hotspot@home service [27] is an example of a real-world service that performs adaptations according to changes in its context information. In this service, a mobile phone's voice communication application is able to seamlessly switch the communication channel between a cellular network link and a WiFi connection when the user enters any of T-Mobile hotspot's coverage area. However, this solution is limited to adaptation at the protocol-layer for voice communication, and only recognizes network domains provided by T-Mobile. Hence, any additional or similar service would have to be developed from scratch. Since neither the service is general purpose nor is based on a framework for context-aware computing, that solution does not easily apply to another context-based adaptation. In fact, only location-aware applications have been widely deployed, producing some commercial products. However, these are still heavily based on applications and specific technologies.

1.2 Requirements and Challenges

In Weiser's ubiquitous computing vision [30], applications should be able to seamlessly interact with distributed context management systems, without compromising the consistency of their interests. However, application's interests may need to be adapted or reinterpreted when the running environment suffers a change, as a consequence of addition of new sensors ou by device's migration, for instance. Kindberg and Fox [22] call this requirement of spontaneous interoperation. A middleware for such a scenario must fulfill five basic requirements: (i) distributed context management, (ii) uniform representation of context interests, (iii) support for seamless evolution of context management systems, (iv) dynamic context discovery, and (v) domains of context perception.

In a macro-scale ubiquitous scenario, a context management system must be distributed in order to allow efficient and scalable dissemination of context. However, a distributed architecture may introduce new problems for context-aware applications, as it requires prior knowledge of the entity of the distributed middleware infrastructure that is responsible for disseminating a specific context they are interested in. Thus, distributed context management must be implemented in conjunction with services for dynamic discovery of context management systems and for transparent distribution of context information.

Multiple environments and administrative domains may use different representations and specializations for the same type of context information, according to the particularities of each environment and their context providers. For example, location information may have various representations [17] such as physical (e.g., geographic), symbolic or relative position, and it may be provided by a different sort of sensors such as GPS, Active Badges [29] or inference agents (e.g. [23]). Some of these context providers are device-embedded sensors, while others are provided by services executing in the wired network infrastructure. An application that tracks the location of some portable devices, whose position may be provided by various sensors placed in different environments, needs to describe an interest that comprehends each possible type of location information (e.g., GPS coordinates, relative location, symbolic location). This requirement is called *uniform description of context interests*.

Furthermore, context-aware environments are inherently dynamic as a result of frequent replacement and addition of new types of sensors, applications or context inference mechanisms. As a result, these changes may require adaptations on the context models, the context databases, or in the means that the middleware processes context interests. The main challenge here is therefore to accommodate such changes on the environment without compromising active context interests. If an application or middleware cannot deal with such evolution of the environment, then the application's interest is likely to become inconsistent and invalid during its lifespan, causing disruptions in previously specified interests. In addition, the creation or change of context types must not compromise the consistency of global context type systems.

A distributed context-aware infrastructure may offer context data of different types and sources that essentially describe the same context information that an application is interested in. The selection of which data type is most appropriate for the application's purpose may depend on the context meta-attributes, such as precision and accuracy, and may dynamically change accordingly to the availability of new context providers. For example, when a device enters a new physical environment that has its own location mechanism, applications interested in this device's location should become aware of the availability of this new type of location information and should evaluate if this new type of location is appropriate for their purposes. Ideally, the middleware, instead of the application, should be responsible for choosing the most adequate context information among a dynamic set of available ones. This requirement is called *dynamic context discovery*.

Finally, the usage of certain context information may be restricted to some domains, environments or applications. In this case, by restricting the access and *perception* of the context, we may increase the scalability of the middleware. Moreover, it reduces the number of CMSs that may be involved in the conflict resolution of multiple context interests. This requirement is compliant with the principle of system boundary [22] of ubiquitous applications.

These five requirements call not only for a new middleware architecture, but also for primitives for describing context interests.

1.3 Limitation of Current Approaches

In classical approaches to context-aware computing, such as ContextToolkit [11], CMSs are isolated and independent from each other, and do not support means of communication amongst each other. These isolated environments are like *context-aware islands*, because they hinder the implementation of applications with global or cross-environment interest in context information, i.e., applications whose context interest is a combination of several pieces of contextual information provided in different environments. Such systems are typically conceived to operate independently, based on their own restricted view of the world [8]. In those systems, the responsibility to implement contextual interoperability is delegated to applications.

Some middleware systems try to overcome the aforementioned limitations by offering either distributed platforms for context management [3, 12, 14, 19], federations of context management systems [2, 9, 21], peer-to-peer interaction approaches [24, 26], or bridges [16] among context management systems. The first approach concentrates on allowing efficient dissemination of context information among distributed clients, which is, however, only one of the requirements in a distributed scenario. The second and the last approaches support interoperability among different administrative domains. Although they implement important requirements of this scenario, they do not properly support other aspects, such as system scalability, generality and environment's evolution.

In a truly ubiquitous scenario, where a mobile application must be able to adapt to diverse CMSs as the user roams through different domains, the adoption of these middleware approaches for context-aware computing has several drawbacks. Firstly, applications need a global knowledge of each available CMS in order to identify which one provides the context information they require. If more than one CMS contains the desired information, applications must dynamically solve potential type conflicts and inconsistencies among different context types and providers, and decide which context information is the most appropriate for their current task. Such adaptivity requirement usually increases application's complexity. Finally, in dynamic and evolvable context-aware systems, updates of context models and providers normally cause disruption of the application's access to context information, if they are bound only statically to previously known CMS or are able to handle only specific types of context information.

Hence, the problem of context management in distributed and dynamic environments has three main aspects to consider: support for *heterogeneity* [6, 7] specially in terms of sensors, applications and context models that are provided in an environment; support for the *environment's evolution* avoiding disruptions in application's behavior; and support for *scalability*, in terms of the number of context types and the context-aware applications. Clearly, there is a trade-off among these three aspects and, in fact, there is no a single solution that adequately satisfies all of these requirements.

1.4 Goals

This book argues that in distributed and dynamic environments, context-aware applications require *context interest of variable wideness*, i.e. interest that involves an undefined set of CMSs or an undefined set of context types.

The goal of this book is to present a middleware architecture for context management that enables the combination of dynamic and evolvable context management systems. As a result, applications can describe and maintain a context interest that involves context provided by various environments, independently of the environment where the user is currently located.

To achieve this goal, this book proposes a novel organization of distributed context management systems based on the concept of *context domains*.

1.5 Summary of Contributions

The main contributions of the work presented in this book are:

- The concept of *context domains* as an approach to compose distributed context management systems, so that applications may maintain context interests across systems.

- Development of a primitive for describing a context interest of variable wideness in context information distributed through context domains. This primitive enables applications to describe either a broad or a narrow interest that addresses simultaneously the application's purposes, the environment scope, and the distributed nature of the context providers.
- A distributed middleware that implements the aforementioned concepts, without compromising scalability and efficiency of context access. This middleware allows the development of context-aware applications at mobile devices, and runs on two mobile device platforms: Android and Java J2ME CDC 1.1.

1.6 Organization of this Book

This book is organized as follows. Chapter 2 describes the problem of managing context-aware applications in distributed and dynamic environments, which is the focus of this book. Chapter 3 describes the state-of-the-art middleware systems and infrastructures for context management and discusses their drawbacks when used on the proposed ubiquitous scenarios. Chapter 4 describes the central idea of the book: the definition of hierarchically context domains to organize distributed CMSs. Chapter 5 presents a full scenario of an application dynamically interacting with distributed CMSs using the proposed approach. Chapter 6 presents a middleware architecture that enables the implementation of the context domain concept. Chapter 7 presents the evaluation of the middleware and the validation of the proposed solution. Finally, Chap. 8 summarizes the contributions of the work presented in this book and presents future research work.

References

1. Bolchini, C., Curino, C.A., Quintarelli, E., Schreiber, F.A., Tanca, L.: A data-oriented survey of context models. Sigmod Rec. **36**(4), 19–26 (2007). doi:10.1145/1361348.1361353
2. Buchholz, T., Krause, M., Linnhoff-Popien, C., Schiffers, M.: CoCo: dynamic composition of context information. In: First Annual International Conference on Mobile and Ubiquitous Systems: Networking and Services (MobiQuitous'04), pp. 335–343 (2004)
3. Chen, G., Li, M., Kotz, D.: Design and implementation of a large-scale context fusion network. In: The First Annual International Conference on Mobile and Ubiquitous Systems: Networking and Services, Mobiquitous 2004, pp. 246–255 (2004). doi:10.1109/MOBIQ.2004.1331731
4. Chen, H.: An intelligent broker architecture for pervasive context-aware systems. Ph.D. thesis, University of Maryland, Baltimore County (2004)
5. Chen, H., Finin, T.W., Joshi, A.: Using OWL in a pervasive computing broker. In: Workshop on Ontologies in Open Agent Systems (OAS), pp. 9–16. Melbourne, Australia (2003)
6. da Rocha, R.C.A., Endler, M.: Evolutionary and efficient context management in heterogeneous environments. In: MPAC'05: Proceedings of the 3rd International Workshop on Middleware for Pervasive and Ad-Hoc Computing, pp. 1–7. ACM Press, New York (2005). doi:10.1145/1101480.1101487

7. da Rocha, R.C.A., Endler, M.: Context management in heterogeneous, evolving ubiquitous environments. IEEE Distrib. Syst. Online 7(4) (2006), Art. no. 0604–o4001
8. Davies, N., Gellersen, H.W.: Beyond prototypes: challenges in deploying ubiquitous systems. IEEE Pervasive Comput. 1(1), 26–35 (2002). doi:10.1109/MPRV.2002.993142
9. Dearle, A., Kirby, G.N.C., Morrison, R., McCarthy, A., Mullen, K., Yang, Y., Connor, R.C.H., Welen, P., Wilson, A.: Architectural support for global smart spaces. In: Proceedings of the 4th International Conference on Mobile Data Management, MDM '03, pp. 153–164. Springer, London (2003)
10. Dey, A.K.: Providing architectural support for building context-aware applications. Ph.D. thesis, College of Computing, Georgia Institute of Technology (2000)
11. Dey, A.K., Abowd, G.D., Salber, D.: A conceptual framework and a toolkit for supporting the rapid prototyping of context-aware applications. Hum. Comput. Interact. 16(2–4), 97–166 (2001). doi:10.1207/S15327051HCI16234_02
12. Gibbons, P., Karp, B., Ke, Y., Nath, S., Seshan, S.: Irisnet: an architecture for a worldwide sensor web. IEEE Pervasive Comput. 2(4), 22–33 (2003). doi:10.1109/MPRV.2003.1251166
13. Grossmann, M., Bauer, M., Honle, N., Kappeler, U.P., Nicklas, D., Schwarz, T.: Efficiently managing context information for large-scale scenarios. In: Third IEEE International Conference on Pervasive Computing and Communications, PerCom 2005, pp. 331–340 (2005). doi:10.1109/PERCOM.2005.17
14. Henricksen, K., Indulska, J., McFadden, T., Balasubramaniam, S.: Middleware for distributed context-aware systems. Lect. Notes Comput. Sci. 3760, 846–863 (2005)
15. Henricksen, K., Indulska, J., Rakotonirainy, A.: Modeling context information in pervasive computing systems. In: Proceedings of the First International Conference on Pervasive Computing, Pervasive '02, pp. 167–180. Springer, London (2002)
16. Hesselman, C., Benz, H., Pawar, P., Liu, F., Wegdam, M., Wibbles, M., Broens, T., Brok, J.: Bridging context management systems for different types of pervasive computing environments. In: First International Conference on Mobile Wireless Middleware, Operating Systems and Applications (MOBILWARE). ACM Press, Innsbruck, (2008)
17. Hightower, J., Borriello, G.: Location systems for ubiquitous computing. Computer 34(8), 57–66 (2001). doi:10.1109/2.940014
18. Hong, J.I., Landay, J.A.: An infrastructure approach to context-aware computing. Hum. Comput. Interact. 16(2–4), 287–303 (2001)
19. Hong, J.I., Landay, J.A.: An architecture for privacy-sensitive ubiquitous computing. In: Proceedings of the 2nd International Conference on Mobile Systems, Applications, and Services, MobiSys '04, pp. 177–189. ACM Press, New York (2004). doi:10.1145/990064.990087
20. Julien, C., Roman, G.C.: EgoSpaces: facilitating rapid development of context-aware mobile applications. IEEE Trans. Softw. Eng. 32(5), 281–298 (2006). doi:10.1109/TSE.2006.47
21. Kiani, S.L., Riaz, M., Zhung, Y., Lee, S., Lee, Y.K.: A distributed middleware solution for context awareness in ubiquitous systems. In: 11th IEEE International Conference on Embedded and Real-Time Computing Systems and Applications (RTCSA'05), pp. 451–454. IEEE Computer Society, Los Alamitos, CA, USA (2005). doi:10.1109/RTCSA.2005.9
22. Kindberg, T., Fox, A.: System software for ubiquitous computing. IEEE Pervasive Comput. 1(1), 70–81 (2002). doi:10.1109/MPRV.2002.993146
23. Nascimento, F.N.d.C.: A service for location inference of mobile devices based on IEEE 802.11. Master's thesis, Departamento de Informática, PUC-Rio (2006). (in portuguese)
24. Riva, O.: Contory: A middleware for the provisioning of context information on smart phones. In: ACM/IFIP/USENIX 7th International Middleware Conference (Middleware'06). Melbourne (Australia) (2006)
25. Roman, M., Hess, C., Cerqueira, R., Ranganathan, A., Campbell, R., Nahrstedt, K.: A middleware infrastructure for active spaces. IEEE Pervasive Comput. 1(4), 74–83 (2002). doi:10.1109/MPRV.2002.1158281
26. Springer, T., Kadner, K., Steuer, F., Yin, M.: Middleware support for context-awareness in 4g environments. In: Proceedings of the 2006 International Symposium on on World of Wireless, Mobile and Multimedia Networks, WOWMOM '06, pp. 203–211. IEEE Computer Society, Washington, DC (2006). doi:10.1109/WOWMOM.2006.71

27. The New York Times: T-Mobile tests dual wi-fi and cell service. Home Page (2006). Accessed 28 June 2008
28. van Kranenburg, H., Bargh, M., Iacob, S., Peddemors, A.: A context management framework for supporting context-aware distributed applications. IEEE Commun. Mag. **44**(8), 67–74 (2006). doi:10.1109/MCOM.2006.1678112
29. Want, R., Hopper, A., Falcao, V., Gibbons, J.: The active badge location system. ACM Trans. Inf. Syst. **10**(1), 91–102 (1992). doi:10.1145/128756.128759
30. Weiser, M.: Some computer science issues in ubiquitous computing. Commun. ACM **36**(7), 75–84 (1993). doi:10.1145/159544.159617
31. Yau, S.S., Karim, F., Wang, Y., Wang, B., Gupta, S.K.S.: Reconfigurable context-sensitive middleware for pervasive computing. IEEE Pervasive Comp. **1**(3), 33–40 (2002)

Chapter 2
Foundations of Context Management in Distributed and Dynamic Environments

Abstract Context information is data that describes the state of a certain entity at a specific moment. A context management system is a computational element responsible for binding context providers, which produce context information, and context consumers, typically represented by context-aware applications. The main task of a context management system is to match consumer's interests with probed context information. The complexity of context management in a distributed scenario is defined by the wideness of an interest, i.e. the number of context management systems that should be involved in an interest matching. If a distributed scenario is also open, heterogeneous and dynamic, than the wideness of an interest is variable, as a result of characteristics such as dynamic introduction of new sensors and evolution of context models. The support of context interest of variable wideness imposes challenging requirements for context management systems.

Keywords Distributed context management · Context-aware computing · Middleware · Open distributed systems

2.1 Introduction

In context-aware applications, adaptations are triggered by changes of certain context information. For example, smart applications designed to support meetings may automatically transfer a presentation to a projector as soon as the presenter enters the meeting room [5]. In this case, both the location of the presenter and his/her role in the meeting room are basic pieces of context information used to trigger the transfer of the presentation. Basically, the development of a context-aware application, as in this example, involves the description of the actions to be triggered according to a set of contextual conditions.

R. C. A. da Rocha and M. Endler, *Context Management for Distributed and Dynamic*   9
Context-Aware Computing, SpringerBriefs in Computer Science,
DOI: 10.1007/978-1-4471-4020-7_2, © The Author(s) 2012

A same piece of context information may be used for different purposes. The location of the presenter, for example, may also be used by another application to disseminate his availability status for an instant communicator. Moreover, this context information may be provided by different sensors, such as a proximity sensor to identify if the user is inside the classroom and using a microphone connected to a voice recognition software to identify specific users in the classroom, as in [22]. This requirement of reuse calls for middleware systems to enable context-aware computing, instead of requiring that applications be developed from scratch.

The main goal of middleware in context-aware computing is to enable decoupled communication between sensors that provide context data and applications interested in context information. Most middleware systems have developed mechanisms that ease incorporation of sensors (e.g., ContextToolkit [6]), and enable high-level description of context conditions that applications are interested in, thus avoiding applications having to poll sensors. Typically, these middleware systems adopt asynchronous communication mechanisms, such as publish/subscribe [7] or tuple-space systems [23], as the basis of interactions among sensors and applications. These mechanisms allow applications to register interests in context information and to asynchronously receive notifications of events that match their interests. RCSM [24], Confab [13], PACE [10] and MoCA [19] are examples of middleware systems that adopt such communication paradigm. Even higher-level programming abstractions for context-aware computing, such as *profiles* [24] and *preferences* [9], require lower-level mechanisms based on asynchronous notifications. In fact, asynchronous communication is the most elementary mechanism of context-aware middleware systems, which is in charge of three main tasks: storage of context information, management of application's subscriptions, and dissemination of events that represent a situation of interest. Some systems delegate this management task to general-purpose asynchronous event systems, which constitutes the context management layer of most middleware systems, as proposed by Henricksen and Indulska [9]. However, general-purpose asynchronous systems do not satisfy adequately the requirements to enable context-aware computing in a distributed and dynamic scenario. In general, publish/subscribe systems focus only on efficient event dissemination and routing in a distributed scenario.

This chapter discusses this challeging problem using the following organization. Section 2.2 defines the foundational concepts of context management. Sections 2.3 and 2.4 present the conceptual layers of context interest management and discusses challenges of enabling context management in a distributed and dynamic environment, respectively. These challenges call for a new class of context interest called *interest of variable wideness*, as presented in Sect. 2.4.2.

2.2 General Concepts

In order to exemplify the general concepts of context-aware computing, consider the following running example:

> *UMessenger* is a location-aware messaging application that enables communication of a user with a group of people (his buddies), integrating functionalities of a mobile phone and of an instantaneous communicator. By knowing the position of his/her buddies on a map, the user can initiate location-oriented interactions based on their location. The user can also define location-based notification conditions, e.g., "tell me when buddy x arrives at home". The location of the user and his/her buddies are obtained from GPS sensors on their devices. The map is obtained from a geolocation map service. *UMessenger* has also the ability to adapt the communication mechanism (e.g. voice, video, asynchronous and synchronous messages) to the current device's network connectivity.

2.2.1 Context, Entity, Types and Instances

In a context-aware application, any interaction is based on two elementary concepts: *entity* and *context information*, as defined below.

> Entity is any object that has a state and that can be represented in a computational environment, such as a physical object, a user, or computational resource.

> Context Information is an abstract information that describes the state of an entity.

In the *UMessenger* example, *location* and *network connectivity* are pieces of context information that characterizes the state of the entity *user device*. Hence, the device's state at a specific instant could be: *(location = home)* and *(network connectivity = using wired network)*. For the sake of simplicity, consider that the user's device location in fact represents the user's location. This definition of context information is consistent to the definition already proposed by Dey [6]. Context-aware systems implement context information through *context types* and *instances* of these types.

> Context type is a computational implementation of a context information which specifies, at least, its data structure.

For example, to represent the data provided by the GPS sensor, the *UMessenger* may implement a `GPSLocation` type composed of three float numbers: *latitude*, *longitude* and *elevation*.

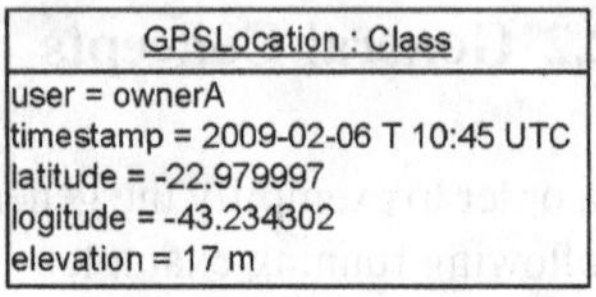

Fig. 2.1 Example of a
Context Instance

GPSLocation : Class
user = ownerA
timestamp = 2009-02-06 T 10:45 UTC
latitude = -22.979997
logitude = -43.234302
elevation = 17 m

A middleware may adopt various types to represent an abstract context information. For example, location may have various representations [12], such as symbolic location [17] (e.g., *RoomA*, *BuildingFPLF*) and proximity-based location [18]. As a result, each representation could be modeled in a particular context type. However, an application may be only prepared to deal with some of these types. For example, if the *UMessenger* is prepared only to display the location on a map based on geo coordinates, then a location sensor that provides symbolic location will not be useful for this application.

This book uses the term *context instance* to describe a piece of data that contains context information, as defined below.

Context instance is a value or an aggregate of values that describes the state of an entity at a specific instant of time and which conforms to a certain *context type*. A context instance i is an object of context type T defined by the tuple $C_i^T = (e, t, V_T)$, where
- e: the entity.
- t: a timestamp.
- V_T: a set of values for each attribute defined in type T.

A GPSLocation instance could be described by the tuple shown in Figure 2.1. A context instance is a snapshot of the state of an entity, at a specific instant of time. The relationship between a context type and an instance is similar to the relationship between a class and an object in the object-oriented programming paradigm. Although the concept of *context information* is an abstraction of *context instance*, for an implementation of a context-aware system, these two terms can be used interchangeably.

2.2.2 Context Model and Modeling Approach

Context Model A context model determines the set of all context types and entities, and relationships among them.

The definition of a context model is a part of the implementation of a context-aware system. A context model defines relevant concepts to the application domain, which the middleware is prepared to deal with. For example, the CoBrA middleware [5] models entities such as *Agent*, *Person*, *Meeting*, *Event* and *Schedule*, which are the basis of the implementation of smart meeting applications. In the case of

UMessenger, since the application basically deals with location and resources of a device, the application should adopt a model that, at least, describes context types to represent *location* and *resources*, as well as an entity type to represent *devices*.

The expressiveness and complexity of a context model depends on the *modeling approach* adopted in the system, which defines how the concepts and their relationships are described. We define context modeling approach as follow.

Context Modeling Approach is the schema used to describe concepts and their relationships in a context model.

A context modeling approach also defines the kinds of relationships a model may support and the meaning of each relationship. An example of a simple context modeling approach is the pair key-value schema, which uses tuples of pairs (*key*, *value*) to describe context information, as adopted in [20]. Using this modeling approach, an instance of GPSLocation would be described by the following set of pairs: ((*latitude* = −22.979997), (*longitude* = −43.234302), (*elevation* = 17)).

Other examples of context modeling approaches [2, 21] are markup schema, graphical, object-oriented, logic based, ontology based and hybrid approaches (e.g. [11]), as discussed in [1].

Some modeling approaches support the formal description of how a context information is inferred from previous existing information. For example, ontology-based approaches use first-order logic to describe how a concept may be inferred from another concept.

2.2.3 Context Providers and Consumers

A context-aware scenario is composed of interations between elements that produce context, called *context providers*, and elements that consume context, called *context consumers*, as defined below.

Context provider is a computational element that populates the context-aware system with context instances of a particular type.

Context consumer is a computational element that consumes context instances to achieve some application-specific purpose.

A *context provider* translates raw data probes obtained from a low-level sensor (e.g., accelerometer, GPS sensor) into context instances on a context model. A provider is a proxy of a sensor in the context-aware system, translating raw data to information that can be used in the system. In the case of *UMessenger*, an application module may be responsible for collecting data from the GPS sensor and for creating the corresponding instances of GPSLocation type. The GPS sensor does not need to know the application's context model, and thus another computational element - the provider - generates the useful data for the application.

Typically, a context consumer is a context-aware application, such as the *UMessenger*, which consumes location information. A computational element may act both as a context consumer and producer, generating a new context information from another lower-level context. For example, some location positioning systems (e.g., [15, 17]) infer a location of a device from triangulation of radio frequency signal strengths from reference points (e.g., 802.11 access points). If such positioning systems model both signal strengths and location as context types, then they infer a context type from another one. This inference is called context reasoning. The external element that produces this reasoning is an inference agent.

Inference Agent is a computational element that consumes context instances to deduce a new context of a different type. The inference agent publishes the resulting context in the system, thus also acting as a context provider.

Hence, an inference agent acts both as a context provider and a consumer.

2.2.4 Contextual Event and Context Interest

A context consumer specifies the situation it is interested in terms of *contextual events* and *context interests*.

Contextual Event is a change in the state of one or more entities that is relevant for some consumer.

For example, the contextual event *phone is offline* could be triggered when the connection with a cellular network is no more available. Upon this event, the *UMessenger* may disable the sending of SMS messages.

Context Interest is a representation of a class of contextual events that a consumer is interested in. A context interest n is defined as a tuple $I_n = (E, T, \varepsilon(V_T))$, where
- E is a set of entities.
- T is the context type
- $\varepsilon(V_T)$ is a boolean function that contains a logic expression based on the values of the attributes V_T. It defines the constraint on context instances that satisfies the interest.

The complexity of $\varepsilon(V_T)$ evaluation depends directly on the context modeling approach adopted. For example, in a middleware that adopts a pair key-value modeling approach, a constraint is a composition of logic expressions based on the values of each attributes (i.e. key).

2.2.5 *Context Selection and Matching*

One of the core responsibilities of a context-aware system is to decide, in a set of context instances, which ones satisfy interests of each consumer, as specified by its *context matching function*. This responsibility still envolves two tasks: *context selection* and *notification composition*.

Context Matching Function is a boolean function $Match(n, i)$ that determines if an context instance i satisfies an interest n.

A context matching function is executed against context instances to check if an instance change must produce a notification for the consumer. Every return *true* results in a notification to a consumer. Basically, a matching function is a translation of interest's $\varepsilon(V_T)$ to the context of the computational element responsible for an interest matching. The complexity of a matching depends directly on the modeling approach adopted. For example, for a pair *key-value* approach, the matching is a comparison of the values of the keys that appear in the interest expression. For an ontology-based approach, the matching is based on the execution of inference on ontology models. In general, the more flexible the matching is, the more complex the implementation of the matching function becomes.

The matching function must be executed when there is a change in the state of an instance, which may correspond to a contextual event.

Context Selection is the task of selecting a subset of context instances to which an interest applies.

A context selection function determines the context instances that should be applied to an interest match, according to the interest specification. In theory of event-based systems, context selection is corresponding to a task called *event filtering* [16]. The complexity of context selection depends on the modeling approach adopted in the system and, in general, defines the class of context the consumer is interested in. Context selection typically depends on the implementation of the underlying asynchronous communication mechanism that a middleware adopts. For example, in a middleware that adopts context management based on a topic-based [7] publish/subscribe system, context selection is based on the topic used in subscriptions. In general, context selection is based on the entity and additional properties of a context interest. In the aforementioned example, the additional property is the topic name.

Notification Composition is the task of choosing the more appropriate notification resulting from an interest match, when more than one context instance satisfies an interest.

Multiple matches may occur when more than one context provider produces the same context information. The resulting information may be complementary or inconsistent, so a consumer must use only one of the notifications to trigger their adaptation. In general, an application may use meta-attributes or quality-of-context information, to select the notification that is more appropriate for an application. For example, an application may specify that it is only interested in the most trustable notification.

Some middleware systems have developed mechanisms to deal with these notification conflicts, such as PACE [10] and CARISMA [3]. When the middleware is responsible for the notification, the interest description must support such meta-attributes. Notification composition may be implemented as a part of the middleware or as an external element, as another middleware component or the application.

2.2.6 Context Management System

A *context management system* (CMS) is an independent computational infrastructure that enables interactions among context providers and consumers, as define below.

Context Management System A context management system (CMS) is an architectural component in context-aware computing responsible for storing context information, published by context providers, and matching previously registered interest to context instances.

A CMS must both store context instances published by providers, as register context interest of consumers, and check them against context instances, thus executing context selection and matching. A CMS is also responsible for managing the context model, validating the consistency of interest and instances according to the model. The underlying modeling approach plays an important role in defining the complexity of implementing the CMS. Depending on the context model approach, management of a model may be resource-intensive. For example, ontology-based models require constant execution of inference rules, which usually degrades the performance of the CMS.

Four main elements characterize a CMS, as illustrated in Fig. 2.2: *primitives*, the *context model*, *context interests*, and *context instances*. Each CMS is responsible for a particular set of context interest and instances, as result of context providers and consumers interacting with it. The CMS's primitives correspond to the interaction paradigm, context modeling approach and the underlying communication middleware on which the CMS is based. An application that interacts with a CMS, is capable for interacting with any other CMS that adopts the same primitives.

Some middleware systems, such as Nexus [8], support heterogeneity among CMS's context models, i.e. each CMS can adopt a particular context model.

Table 2.1 shows the primitives of interaction with a CMS, considering only the asynchronous mode of operation, which is the focus of the work presented in this book.

A CMS may be implemented as a set of distributed infrastructural components, such as proposed in [4]. However, to adhere to the proposed definition, the CMS

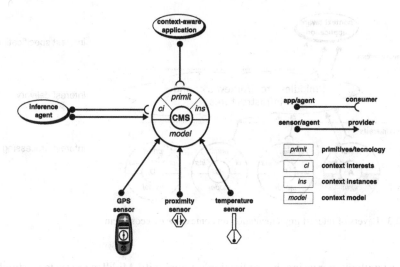

Fig. 2.2 Diagram of a CMS structure and its interaction with providers and consumers

Table 2.1 Main Asynchronous Primitives of Context Management Systems

Operation	Direction	Meaning
publish	Provider → CMS	publishes a context information
registerInterest	Consumer → CMS	registers an interest
notifyMatching	CMS → Consumer	notifies a consumer that a previously registered interest has matched to a context information
unregisterInterest	Consumer → CMS	unregisters a context interest

distribution must be totally transparent for providers and consumers, that address the CMS through the same addressing abstraction. Thus, in the perspective of consumers and providers, there is no difference between accessing distributed CMSs and accessing a unique CMS. Section 2.3 discusses a scenario of distributed CMSs and the role of middleware to confer transparency to such distribution.

2.3 Conceptual Layers of Context Interest Management

The support of context interest in distributed environments, i.e. distributed CMSs, brings up challenges in terms of context management infrastructures and programming abstractions, besides the traditional problems of scalability and distribution[1]. The goal of a middleware for open and evolutionary scenarios is to support context

---

[1] E.g., event notification routing and mobility management.

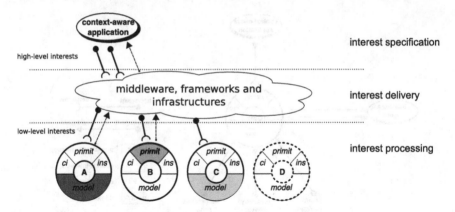

Fig. 2.3 Layers of interest implementation on context-aware ecosystems

interest without increasing the application's complexity. Middleware systems should make transparent the diversity and distribution of a CMS.

Figure 2.3 shows distributed context management systems organized in the conceptual layers. These layers range from the application to CMSs responsible for managing and storing context information. In the figure, the different shading of each CMS's component represents heterogeneity in such aspect among the CMSs. For example, CMSs A, B and C adopt a particular context model, whereas A and C adopt a same primitive which is different from B's primitives. In addition, the different style of CMS C represents that the CMS is not included in the processing of the application's interest.

The *interest specification layer* comprises applications, frameworks and middleware systems that specify and register context interests and that receives notifications when a context data matches an interest. The *interest processing layer* comprises CMSs responsible for storing context information and matching context interests. The *interest delivery layer* comprises middleware infrastructures that route context interests to the corresponding CMS and deliver notifications to the corresponding clients. It also may implement transparent access to distributed CMSs and translate a higher-level interest to lower-level interest. The set of computational elements of all interest layers is called *context-aware ecosystem*.

Several context providers may provide the same context type regarding a specific entity, and those may change dynamically. Thus, an application may need to register its interest on several CMSs that are responsible for that interest, or require that the interest delivery layer translates its high-level interest to the corresponding lower-level interests. The interest translation needs to conform the context model of each CMS, if they are heterogeneous.

The interest delivery layer may also need to implement a distributed notification composition if more than one CMS disseminates notifications for the same interest match. This composition may either be done on the specification layer (application's side) or in the delivery layer. The drawback of the first case is that it increases application complexity.

Consider the case of *UMessenger*. To obtain the updated location of each buddy, the application needs to register in any CMS that stores the location of a buddy. Peer-to-peer messaging applications tipically obtain references to peers to connect and their current connectivity states from a centralized server. This architecture could be suitable for *UMessenger* if location is limited to a GPS embedded sensor. However, a distributed scenario for context management suggests the implementation of a more flexible application, which we call *UMessenger 2.0*, as described below.

UMessenger 2.0 is an extension of *UMessenger* that can work with flexible semantics of location information and different location providers. In the default mode of operation, *UMessenger 2.0* obtains a map from a centralized map provider, as in the previous application version. In this mode, *UMessenger 2.0* describes interests for geo locations of all user's buddies, specifying a preference to obtain location from the most precise provider, which is typically a GPS provider. If GPSLocation is not available, e.g., the user is not using a GPS-enabled device or the user is in an indoor environment, the application shows the location using other alternative providers (e.g., E911 and Active Bats). If the location provider is based on an indoor position system, as in Active Bats, the application provides an option to the user to switch the map view to the view directly associated to the provider (e.g., a building map for an indoor positioning system). Then, the application starts showing the buddy's location according to this new map view, so a buddy who is not present in the area covered by the map will not be shown. *UMessenger 2.0* still enables the corresponding location-based notifications, using the *place* semantic of the new map view: instead of geo locations, semantic locations, such as *Room510* and *5thFloor*. When required, the user can switch to the previous or another map view. *UMessenger 2.0* still maintains the ability to adapt the communication mechanism (e.g., voice, video, async/synchronous messages) to the current device's network connectivity.

In this scenario, an application may need to specify broader or narrower interests, in terms of the CMS involved in the resolution and the context types that satisfy the interest. The complexity of managing an application depends on how broad are its context interests. An interest is more abstract if it involves context managed in more CMSs and if its type is implemented by specific means in more than one CMS. For example, an interest in the Location of a Person p is more abstract than an interest in the GPSLocation of a Buddy p of user u, although both contexts may describe locations of the same person p. Whenever interests are more abstract, applications may need to specify more context interests at different CMSs to describe the condition that triggers the intended adaptation. Such concepts may need to be translated to context model of each CMS. Consequently, the notification composition involves more interest matches.

2.4 Context Interest Management in a Dynamic Context-Aware Ecosystem

In a dynamic context-aware ecosystem, the components of each interest layer may change, as the result of the evolution of the whole ecosystem. Such changes may compromise the consistency of interests and cause disruptions in a context-aware interaction. The main issue regarding this scenario is how to support a context interest that involves more that one CMS. Composing isolated CMSs do not enable to deal with the challenges of this scenario with efficiency and achieving scalability. Furthermore, by supporting a dynamic ecosystem, instead of just isolated CMSs, applications may describe more complex interests. As the ecosystem grows in size, the complexity of dealing with context interests increases, since CMSs may be dynamically introduced or changed.

Five characteristics make challeging the implementation of distributed and dynamic context-aware ecosystems:

- Dynamic deployment of new context providers,
- Dynamic deployment of new context types,
- Scoping of context models,
- Lack of in-advance knowledge of CMS, and
- Dynamic deployment of new CMSs.

The following paragraphs discuss each of these characteristics.

Dynamic Deployment of New Context Providers

New sensors may be constantly introduced in the ecosystem, as a result of the development of new devices, more precise sensors, new sensing mechanisms or new inference mechanisms. If a new sensor provides context involved in an interest, then it must be included in the interest matching. From the point of view of an application, perceiving a new sensor means to have the provided context included in the interest selection and matching. On the matching of interests, running applications with alive interests should be able to recognize the new provider, without requiring them to be restarted, recompiled or redeveloped.

The need to perceive a sensor may be the result of client mobility. For example, if a device enters in a physical environment that provides location sensors, than any context consumer interested in the device's location must have its interests also registered in the corresponding CMS.

Table 2.2 Example of context location providers (sensors) and the placement of their CMS

Provider	CMS Location	Applicability
GPS	Locally placed	Outdoor
E911	Cellular network	Indoor/Outdoor
ActiveBadges	Building infrastructure	Indoor

Dynamic Deployment of Context Types

As the result of the introduction of new sensors, the context model may also need to conform to particularities of the new provided context information. For example, location sensors that provide geographic coordinates and relative location must have different representations in the context model. Although both describe a location, the structure of the provided context is completely different. If a consumer can deal with the information of the new provider/type, then his/her active interests for an already existing type must include the new type in the interest matching.

Scoping of Context Models

Applications should be prepared to describe context interests based on various context models, and some of them may be restricted or relevant only within their administrative domains. The heterogeneity of CMS's context models is also desirable, since it promotes efficiency and security.

Lack of In-Advance Knowledge of CMS

For some interests, the CMSs responsible for managing the context can be statically discovered. For example, both a GPS sensor and an accelerometer are internal device sensors, so applications may be statically prepared to collect and deal with context information they provide. For other providers, however, a consumer does not know previously the CMSs that contain the desired context and, thus, where its interests must be registered. For example, there may be many CMSs, as Table 2.2 exemplifies, each one from a different administrative domain, that provide a particular location information for some users. If the context-aware ecosystem requires that all consumers make an explicit addressing of CMSs where their interest has be registered, then applications should be developed to have a previous knowledge of existing CMSs. In a highly distributed ecosystem, dealing with all CMSs may introduce a heavy burden to applications, which have to deal with an amount of interest registry and the composition of the resulting notification matches.

The interest delivery layer plays an important role to identify the CMSs where a specific consumer interest must be registered.

Dynamic Deployment of CMSs

As a result of the incremental introduction of context-aware computing, new CMSs may be dynamically deployed and start participating in the ecosystem. This fact introduces a more challenging scenario in terms of addressing and delivering interests to CMS, discussed in the previous characteristic.

These five characteristics produce a dynamic and unpredictable behavior on the interest processing layer. A middleware for context-aware computing should deal with such dynamics, keeping it transparent to the upper level interest description layer. In fact, the challenges for the implementation of dynamic context-aware ecosystems, relates both in the interest delivery layer and in the interest description layer. The following sections discuss the resulting middleware requirements for the layer of interest delivery and interest description.

2.4.1 Requirements of the Interest Delivery Layer

A middleware that supports dynamic context-aware ecosystems must satisfy five requirements: (i) support for seamless evolution of context management systems, (ii) dynamic context discovery, (iii) domains of context perception, (iv) uniform representation of context interests, and (v) distributed context management.

The interest delivery layer directly handles changes of the elements of the interest processing layer, as result of the dynamic deployment of CMSs, sensors, and types (context model). Hence, the interest delivery layer is responsible for accommodating such changes for the currently active context interests, without the need to restart or invalidate registered context interests, i.e. supporting seamlessly the evolution of context management systems.

This dynamics within an ecosystem also requires the dynamic discovery of CMSs. For example, in *UMessenger 2.0*, to track the location of a specific buddy, the interest delivery layer must register the application's interest at the corresponding CMSs that maintain location information for the selected buddy. If the buddy moves to another environment and, as a consequence, sensors connected to other CMSs start publishing the location of the buddy, then the application's interest must be registered at those CMSs. Registering an interest at all available CMSs is not an acceptable approach because the middleware will not scale with the number of application's interests. Ideally, the middleware should dynamically discover which CMSs may contains context involved in a context interest. This book uses the term *dynamic context discovery* to express this requirement.

A middleware for context management must support *domains of context perception*, i.e. must allow each CMS to adopt a particular context model. In addition, the middleware must be aware of this model heterogeneity among CMSs, and then register an interest at the CMSs for which it applies. Also, in this case, the middleware would not scale if the whole ecosystem is based on a single context model.

Table 2.3 Mapping between requirement for context management middleware and Kindberg and Fox's principle for ubiquitous computing

Requirement	Related Principles
Support for seamless evolution of context-aware management systems	Volatility
Dynamic context discovery	Volatility & System boundary
Domains of context perception	System Boundary
Uniform Interest Description	Spontaneous Interoperation
Distributed Context Management	Scalability & System boundary

The dynamics of the ecosystem calls for heterogeneous CMSs, specially in terms of models and managed sensors. The middleware must adopt a primitive to describe context interests that can be the interpreted and registered at any CMS, in spite of their heterogeneity. This requirement is called *uniform representation of context interests*.

Finally, since an ecosystem is inherently composed of distributed CMSs, the middleware also must support distributed context management.

These five requirements are aligned with the following three principles of Kindberg and Fox [14] for system software for ubiquitous computing:

- *Volatility*: the set of participating users, hardware, and software is highly dynamic and unpredictable.
- *System boundary*: an ecosystem is divided into environments with boundaries that demarcate their content, creating the notion of environment's scope.
- *Spontaneous interoperation*: software components may spontaneously enter in the ecosystem and start interactions with each other.

In fact, the goal of proposed approach for context management is to promote ubiquity in a dynamic context-aware ecosystem. In addition to Kindberg and Fox's principle, a context-aware ecosystem also demands for *scalability* as an orthogonal principle. Table 2.3 shows the relationship between each discussed requirement for a context management middleware and the corresponding principle proposed by Kindberg and Fox.

2.4.2 Requirements for Interest Description Layer

The characteristics of a distributed and dynamic context-aware ecosystem may impact on the complexity of a context interest. For example, an application may need to describe the specific CMS to which an interest applies. In this case, the CMS assumes the meaning of the interest's scope.

In contrast, if an interest is not explicitly restricted to a particular CMS then the set of CMSs responsible for its processing cannot be solved *in interest description time*. In a context-aware ecosystem, each CMS may have a particular context model,

Table 2.4 Classification of Context Interest Expressions

Aspect	Type	Description
Domain of CMS	Closed domain (D_C)	Expression applies to a specific (and well-known) CMS.
		Ex: *Application adapts its mode of communication according to device resources (local domain).*
	Relative domain (D_R)	Expression only applies to the current CMS to which an application or the contextualized entity is associated.
		Ex: *Obtain the map of the current domain.*
	Open domain (D_O)	Expression must be applied to a broader domain space of CMS.
		Ex: *UMessenger 2.0uses location obtained from any provider to track the user's buddy location.*
Type Coverage	Specific Type (T_S)	Expression applies to a very specific and previously known context type.
		Ex: *UMessenger 2.0uses wireless bandwidth to adapt its communication mechanisms/protocol.*
	Abstract Type (T_A)	Interest expression applies to a general and abstract context type, which may be specialized by different and specific context types, that in turn is provided by different context sources.
		Ex: *UMessenger 2.0requests abstract location to locate a user in a map, which may be either a coordinate-based location or a symbolic location.*

as a result of the particularities of the corresponding environment. Consequently, a type involved in a specific interest may be recognized only in a subset of ecosystem's CMSs. Thus, the CMSs that process an interest may range from a particular one to the whole ecosystem's CMSs. We call *wideness* of an interest such behavior of being more broad or more narrow. The set of CMSs that recognizes a certain context type must be evaluated at runtime, so we say that a context-aware ecosystem enables *context interests of variable wideness*, as defined below.

Context interest of variable wideness is a context interest in a context-aware ecosystem that either involves an undefined number of CMSs in its matching or undefined actual context types.

Table 2.4 classifies context interest expressions according to two orthogonal aspects: *domains of CMS*, i.e. which set of CMS may be involved in a context interest resolution, and *type coverage*, i.e. how specific is the context type which the application is interested in. Table 2.4 also shows some examples of these interests, using *UMessenger 2.0* as a reference.

The *domain of CMS* specifies which of the CMSs will participate in the processing of a context interest. Since more than one CMS may contain providers for the same type of context information, a context interest may require the registration of lower-level interests at several CMSs. Then the interest must be disseminated to each CMS and the corresponding notifications must be delivered back to the application. If an interest specifies exactly one CMS responsible for its processing, then we say that it is a closed domain (D_C) interest.

However, in a distributed and open scenario, where new CMSs and context providers may be added and removed at anytime, an application may not be able to identify the set of CMSs that provide a specific context. In this case, if a change occurs at runtime, it may cause inconsistencies or disruptions in interest match notifications. When an interest must be applied to an undefined set of CMSs, we call this expression of an open domain (D_O) interest. A relative domain expression (D_R) is a particular case of interest where it must be applied only to the closest scope of CMS to which the application or the contextualized entity is associated.

The other aspect of interest expression is the scope of the context type requested in an interest expression. In this case, we assume that the system supports hierarchical context models with the notion of super and subtyping among context types. An interest expression associated to an abstract type (T_A) may be refined to interests of any subtype, increasing the number of notifications and the complexity of result interpretation. An expression for a specific type (T_S), defines precisely the actual type that must be involved in an interest match. Distributed and open CMSs increase the complexity of implementing abstract type expression, since they allow each domain to have its own context model.

The goal of a middleware for such an open and evolutionary scenario is to enable those interest expressions without increasing the application's complexity. Middleware systems should make transparent the diversity and distribution of CMS, in terms of context models and available context sources. Furthermore, the middleware's programming abstractions should allow applications to specify in just one context interest expression, D_O interests, leaving for the middleware to solve the inconsistencies among interest match notifications, according to the application requirements.

Chapter 5 presents a case study of an implementation of the *UMessenger 2.0*, discussing in more detail the different types of interest expressions that can be used by the application.

2.5 Summary

This chapter has shown the fundamental concepts for context-aware computing and the main components of an architecture for context-aware computing. This chapter used as a running example a hypothetical application called *UMessenger*. In special, two fundamental concepts were used: context interest and context management system (CMS).

Section 2.3 introduced the term context-aware ecosystem to specify all elements that interact among each other in an architecture of distributed context-aware computing. The management of context interest in an ecosystem is composed of three conceptual layers: interest description, interest delivery, and interest processing layers.

Section 2.4 discussed how the dynamics of a context-aware ecosystem challenges the implementation of management layers of context interests. As a result of this discussion, Sect. 2.4.1 enumerated five requirements for a middleware for distributed context management in respect to interest delivery layer whereas Sect. 2.4.2 argued that in a context-aware ecosystem, applications demand for interest description approach that enable the description of interest with variable domain of CMS and coverage of types. This interest is called *context interest of variable wideness*.

The next chapter presents distributed architectures for context management that integrates and composes distributed CMSs, to build a context-aware ecosystem, and discusses how they support context interests of variable wideness.

References

1. Bettini, C., Brdiczka, O., Henricksen, K., Indulska, J., Nicklas, D., Ranganathan, A., Riboni, D.: A survey of context modelling and reasoning techniques. Pervasive Mob. Comput. **6**(2), 161–180 (2010). doi:10.1016/j.pmcj.2009.06.002
2. Bolchini, C., Curino, C.A., Quintarelli, E., Schreiber, F.A., Tanca, L.: A data-oriented survey of context models. SIGMOD Rec. **36**(4), 19–26 (2007). doi:10.1145/1361348.1361353
3. Capra, L., Emmerich, W., Mascolo, C.: CARISMA: context-aware reflective middleware system for mobile applications. IEEE Transact. Softw. Eng. **29**(10), 929–945 (2003). doi:10.1109/TSE.2003.1237173
4. Chen, G., Li, M., Kotz, D.: Design and implementation of a large-scale context fusion network. In: The First Annual International Conference on Mobile and Ubiquitous Systems: Networking and Services, Mobiquitous 2004, pp. 246–255 (2004). doi:10.1109/MOBIQ.2004.1331731
5. Chen, H.: An intelligent broker architecture for pervasive context-aware systems. Ph.D. thesis, University of Maryland, Baltimore County (2004)
6. Dey, A.K., Abowd, G.D., Salber, D.: A conceptual framework and a toolkit for supporting the rapid prototyping of context-aware applications. Hum. Comput. Interact. **16**(2–4), 97–166 (2001). doi:10.1207/S15327051HCI16234_02
7. Eugster, P.T., Felber, P.A., Guerraoui, R., Kermarrec, A.M.: The many faces of publish/subscribe. ACM Comput. Surv. **35**(2), 114–131 (2003). doi:10.1145/857076.857078
8. Grossmann, M., Bauer, M., Honle, N., Kappeler, U.P., Nicklas, D., Schwarz, T.: Efficiently managing context information for large-scale scenarios. In: Third IEEE International Conference on Pervasive Computing and Communications, PerCom 2005, pp. 331–340 (2005). doi:10.1109/PERCOM.2005.17
9. Henricksen, K., Indulska, J.: Developing context-aware pervasive computing applications: models and approach. Pervasive and Mobile Computing **2**(1), 37–64 (2006). doi:10.1016/j.pmcj.2005.07.003
10. Henricksen, K., Indulska, J., McFadden, T., Balasubramaniam, S.: Middleware for distributed context-aware systems. Lect. Notes Comput. Sci. **3760**, 846–863 (2005)
11. Henricksen, K., Livingstone, S., Indulska, J.: Towards a hybrid approach to context modelling, reasoning and interoperation. In: 1st International Workshop on Advanced Context Modelling, Reasoning and Management, pp. 54–61. Orlando, Florida (2004)
12. Hightower, J., Borriello, G.: Location systems for ubiquitous computing. Computer **34**(8), 57–66 (2001). doi:10.1109/2.940014

13. Hong, J.I., Landay, J.A.: An architecture for privacy-sensitive ubiquitous computing. In: Proceedings of the 2nd international conference on Mobile systems, applications, and services, MobiSys '04, pp. 177–189. ACM Press, New York (2004). doi:10.1145/990064.990087

14. Kindberg, T., Fox, A.: System software for ubiquitous computing. IEEE Pervasive Comput. 1(1), 70–81 (2002). doi:10.1109/MPRV.2002.993146

15. LaMarca, A., Chawathe, Y., Consolvo, S., Hightower, J., Smith, I., Scott, J., Sohn, T., Howard, J., Hughes, J., Potter, F., Tabert, J., Powledge, P., Borriello, G., Schilit, B.: Place Lab: device positioning using radio beacons in the wild. In: 3rd International Conference on Pervasive Computing. Munich, Germany (2005)

16. Mühl, G., Fiege, L., Pietzuch, P.: Distributed Event-Based Systems. Springer, New York (2006)

17. Nascimento, F.N.D.C.: A service for location inference of mobile devices based on IEEE 802.11. Master's thesis, Departamento de Informática, PUC-Rio (2006)

18. Orr, R.J., Abowd, G.D.: The smart floor: a mechanism for natural user identification and tracking. In: CHI '00 extended abstracts on Human factors in computing systems, pp. 275–276. ACM, New York, (2000). doi:10.1145/633292.633453

19. Sacramento, V., Endler, M., Rubinsztejn, H.K., Lima, L.S., Goncalves, K., do Nascimento, F.N.: MoCA: a middleware for developing collaborative applications for mobile users. IEEE Distrib. Syst. Online 5(10) (2004)

20. Strang, T., Linnhoff-Popien, C.: Service interoperability on context level in ubiquitous computing environments. In: Proceedings of International Conference on Advances in Infrastructure for Electronic Business, Education, Science, Medicine, and Mobile Technologies on the Internet. L'Aquila, Italy. (2003)

21. Strang, T., Linnhoff-Popien, C.: A context modeling survey. In: First International Workshop on Advanced Context Modelling, Reasoning And Management. Nottingham, England (2004)

22. Undercoffer, J., Perich, F., Cedilnik, A., Kagal, L., Joshi, A.: A secure infrastructure for service discovery and access in pervasive computing. Mob. Netw. Appl. 8(2), 113–125 (2003). doi:10.1023/A:1022224912300

23. Wyckoff, P., McLaughry, S., Lehman, T., Ford, D.: TSpaces. IBM Syst. J. 37(3) (1998)

24. Yau, S.S., Karim, F., Wang, Y., Wang, B., Gupta, S.K.S.: Reconfigurable context-sensitive middleware for pervasive computing. IEEE Pervasive Comput. 1(3), 33–40 (2002)

Chapter 3
State of the Art

Abstract Middleware for context management can be classified in four categories: distributed middleware systems, peer-to-peer context management systems, federation-based approaches and bridging approaches. Distributed middleware systems natively support distributed context management systems. Peer-to-peer context management systems creates the idea of distributions through connections between pairs of context management systems Bridging approaches use bridges to enable interoperability between pairs of heterogeneous context management systems. These approaches do not support context interest of variable wideness without compromising either the scalability of context management, the generality of context interests, or evolution of the environment's context providers.

Keywords Distributed context management · Context-aware computing · Distributed architectures

3.1 Introduction

State-of-the-art middleware systems support distributed context-aware computing by using one of the following four approaches to compose distributed CMSs:

- **Distributed middleware systems**: natively support distributed context management by offering primitives to query distributed CMS.
- **Peer-to-peer context management systems**: support distributed context management through peer-to-peer connections between pairs of CMSs.
- **Federation-based approaches**: enable the composition of distributed CMS in federations that offer a uniform primitive to describe interests that involve more than one CMS.
- **Bridging approaches**: enable interoperability by offering bridges between pairs of CMSs, so an application may use primitives of a CMS to describe interests that apply to all further CMSs to which the original CMS has a bridge.

R. C. A. da Rocha and M. Endler, *Context Management for Distributed and Dynamic Context-Aware Computing*, SpringerBriefs in Computer Science, DOI: 10.1007/978-1-4471-4020-7_3, © The Author(s) 2012

Each one of these approaches adopts different assumptions in terms of heterogeneity and integration requirements. Heterogeneity in a context-aware ecosystem is defined by two aspects: model-oriented heterogeneity, i.e. each CMS adopts a particular context model; and CMS heterogeneity, i.e. CMSs are based on different underlying middleware. Usually, CMS heterogeneity implies also model heterogeneity, as the mapping of concepts between two models may not be supported.

This chapter will skip discussions on middleware systems that propose centralized context management (e.g. ContextToolkit [5]) and that do not offer an approach for handling interests that span distributed CMSs. Some systems, such as CFN/Solar [3], support composition of distributed sensors, instead of CMSs. Such systems are out of scope of this book because they address lower-level aspects of context management, and in its approach context consumers are tight coupled to sensor implementations.

Sections 3.2–3.5 discuss the main representative middleware systems for, respectively, distributed middleware systems, peer-to-peer context management systems, federation-based approaches, and bridging approaches. Each of these sections discuss how each of the approaches supports context interests of variable wideness, according to the classification introduced in the previous chapter.

3.2 Distributed Middleware Systems

Several middleware systems (e.g. [9, 15, 18, 20, 24]) have been developed to enable distributed context-aware systems. The support for delivery of interest expressions to multiple CMSs differs according to the underlying assumptions regarding the CMS's characteristics and the mechanisms for delivery of interest. In general, they assume both model and CMS homogeneity in the distributed environment. Figures 3.1 and 3.2 show two interaction architectures between applications and CMSs through distributed middleware systems. In an approach *without* a delivery layer (Fig. 3.1), an application must have a prior knowledge of which CMS stores the context that it wants to consume, and then register its interest. In an approach *with* a delivery layer (Fig. 3.2), an application queries a registry service to obtain a reference to the CMSs where it must register its interest.

3.2.1 Gaia

Gaia [20] is a component-based middleware centered on the concept of *active spaces*. An active space is a physical area where heterogeneous devices, such as PDAs and printers, may discover, auto-configure and dynamically establish interactions among themselves. The goal of Gaia is to enable dynamic environments for smart meeting rooms.

Gaia provides a context service that enables applications to query and to register context interests, an active space repository, and a contextual file system, that ensures that applications and users access their files even when they migrate to another active

Fig. 3.1 Distributed
Approach for integrating
CMSs *without* delivery layer

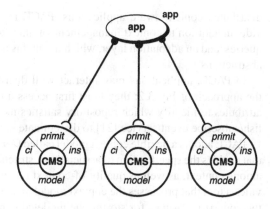

Fig. 3.2 Distributed
Approach for integrating
CMSs *with* delivery layer

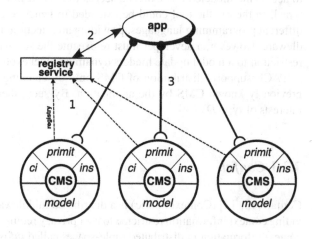

space. When a consumer migrates to another smart space, it loses the access to all context information in its previous smart space, except its files. In fact, Gaia allows applications to move to the domain of another CMS—an *active space* in its terminology—, but requires them to re-apply their context interests to the new domain. Hence, Gaia supports only D_r interests, where the scope of the interest expression is always the current active space to which the consumer is connected with.

3.2.2 PACE

PACE [9] is a middleware developed at University of Queensland, that aims at supporting a highly flexible context model and advanced programming abstractions for distributed context-aware applications. PACE is organized in layers [8] that provide, in addition to context management, an interface to execute distributed context queries, and an adaptation layer, which maintains a reusable repository of adaptation abstractions.

In PACE, applications may interact with distributed context repositories using the approach of Fig. 3.2: they must first access a repository catalogue using meta-attributes to identify which repository satisfies its requirements. PACE uses a publish/subscribe event service [21] to disseminate context to applications.

PACE adopts a flexible context model called Context Modelling Language (CML) that enables the specification of associations, structural restrictions and dependencies among context, as well as quality-of-context parameters [10]. The middleware provides a tool that processes the context model and generates SQL scripts to configure the context repository for storing the modeled context, along with libraries (stubs) to access the modeled context. The access to context information is, thus, strongly typed. In theory, the tool could be extended to generate code to access context in different programming languages, providing architectural independence to the middleware. However, a developer must re-execute the scripts to update a model. This restriction to a model update hinders dynamic model evolution.

PACE supports distribution of CMS only by enabling access to a specific and previously known CMS by the application. By such, they restrict applications to interests of type D_c.

3.2.3 Confab

Confab [13, 14] (Context Fabric) is a distributed middleware that is focused at providing context information restricted to user privacy requirements. Confab maintains context information in distributed tuple-spaces called *infospaces*. Each infospace is a repository responsible for storing one or more context types. An application interested in a certain context, builds a context query using the address of the responsible infospace, using a previously known infospace URIs. Infospace servers maintain groups of infospaces, which in turn may be kept in the device, e.g. if the stored context describes the user's or the device's state.

One or more infospaces correspond to a CMS. However, Confab requires an explicit and static addressing of infospaces, hindering the implementation of D_o interests.

3.2.4 AURA CIS

AURA CIS [6, 15] is another middleware for managing distributed CMS—*context information providers*, according to AURA's concepts. A consumer has access to distributed CMS through a unified interest processor called *CIS Query Synthesizer* that decomposes an interest (a *query*, for AURA) in a set of invocations to distributed CMSs. An interest may contain the following parameters: selected context attributes, provider names, entity selection expression, meta-attribute constraints, and maximum response time.

Like Confab, AURA CIS requires a static deployment of CMS and an explicit addressing of CMS. Since the distributed CMS must be previously known by applications, AURA supports only D_c interests.

3.2.5 Vade

Vade [17, 18] is a middleware to enable ubiquitous applications to access location-aware services in heterogeneous administrative domains. An application seamlessly interacts with services/context of two domains: its home environment and its local (current) environment. Vade infrastructure provides distributed services that enable the implementation of global ubiquitous applications, in terms of this dual-domain supporting approach. Discovery of domains is based on physical location of the applications: Vade uses a Vade directory to map application's current location to the corresponding Vade environment. Hence, Vade supports only D_c interests, where c is always the home environment, and D_r interests.

3.2.6 CMF

Context Management Framework [24] (CMF) enables distributed applications to interact with a distributed context-aware architecture, and, at the same time, providing transparent contextual interoperability for applications. CMF enables applications to seamlessly access distributed context providers.[1] Context discovery is implemented as in PACE: through properties and descriptions stored in a registry, applications and components obtain the address of the context provider that satisfies their requirements. There is no notion of an environment or how it could be translated to registry properties. Moreover, like PACE, CMF does not solve the problem of managing distributed registries. The middleware offers efficient reasoning in a distributed environment through enabling distributed reasoners to access distributed context providers. Context reasoning in CMF is based on ontology reasoning.

---

[1] CMF uses the term *context sources* for providers and *context provider* for CMS.

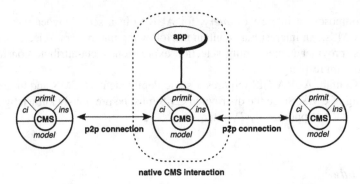

Fig. 3.3 Architecture of peer-to-peer approaches for CMS integration

3.3 Peer-to-Peer Approaches for Context Management

Peer-to-peer approaches to context management require applications (frameworks) or CMSs to establish a direct connection to each CMS that contains context information to be involved in interest matching, as shown in Fig. 3.3. Distribution is generally transparent to applications and, typically, the peer-to-peer connection between two CMS must be constructed before any interest is registered. Hence, peer-to-peer approaches do not support any other interest different of D_c. Contory and the work of Springer et al. are example of such approaches for context management.

3.3.1 Contory

Contory [19] is a middleware for context provision in mobile devices, such as smartphones. Contory's goal is to enable ad hoc collaboration among devices, through the sharing of their context information database. Contory allows the integration of multiple strategies for context provisioning in a framework that keeps transparent the context provider's location (i.e. CMS) to applications (consumers). The CMS integration mechanism is totally transparent to applications, which use a unified query language to describe their context interests.

In Contory, context information is an elementary data associated to a name and which does not entail any typing information. For example, a consumer indicates the name of the context in a query and receives as result the context data. To enable applications to describe interests, the user must previously indicate to Contory which context providers (i.e. CMS for Contory) shall be included in the context information base. Hence, the providers must be statically defined at development time, which thus restricts the interest expressions to class D_c.

3.3.2 Springer et al.'s Work

Springer et al. [22] explored a distributed context management to integrate highly heterogeneous environments based on 4G communication technologies. In the proposed approach, a *ContextManager* manages context information in a specific domain, i.e. a scope of application usage. Multiple domains are integrated through peer-to-peer connections among their *ContextManagers*, which may implement domain-specific[2] APIs.

In a set of domains integrated through peer-to-peer connections, the middleware enables transparent access to context information and description of interests across various distributed domains. However, the approach does not address issues such as evolution, D_r and D_o interests. Moreover, contextual interoperability is based on the adoption of a same top level ontology at each domain.

3.4 Federation-Based Approaches

In federation-based approaches (Fig. 3.4), adopted by middleware systems such as Nexus and CAMUS, there is a mechanism that allows aggregation of independent CMSs by sharing their context models with other CMS and by providing a common interface for applications to interact.

3.4.1 CAMUS

In CAMUS [16], a CMS federation is a set of environments based on CAMUS services, which disseminate context information as tuples. Each tuple is mapped to concepts (i.e. types) through a repository of ontologies, which also enable the inclusion of context reasoners. CAMUS eases the interconnection among inference engines through an architecture of *pluggable reasoning engines*. Each service of an environment is a CMS, that must be registered at a Jini [25] discovery service. A CAMUS context domain is an environment that supports a minimal set of CAMUS services. The set of all Jini services responsible for each CAMUS domain composes a federation. In order to access context information or to use a service of a specific domain, a client must query the Jini federation, using parameters such as the name and localization of the domain.

CAMUS uses the term *context domain* to define an environment that offers context services for a specific domain of usage. To access context from different domains, an application performs Jini lookups to domain services, passing attributes of the required service, such as domain name and physical location. These lookups are

---

[2] i.e. application-specific.

Fig. 3.4 Federation-based
approaches

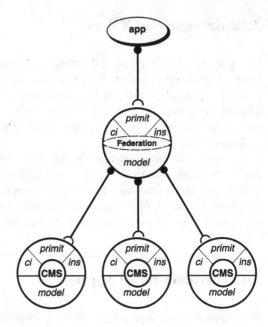

processed by a federation of lookup services for each domain, enabling distributed
queries for context information.

3.4.2 Nexus

In Nexus [7], a federation may contain heterogeneous CMS. In order to allow interoperability among CMSs, each one must implement an abstract interface and register
itself at an *Area Service Register*. A client may access context information provided
by the federation, by using a specific query language. There is no concept such as
domain or environment: each CMS is a repository of a specific context type. Thus
Nexus's CMS heterogeneity is *de facto* type heterogeneity. Consequently, CMS discovery is just a type discovery and neither D_r nor D_c interests are allowed. However,
in Nexus, a new CMS may be dynamically added to a federation, which may allow
applications to execute D_o expressions.

3.4.3 GLOSS

GLOSS [4] implements an approach similar to Nexus: it composes heterogeneous
CMS through hierarchical or peer-to-peer interconnection methods. This flexibility
enables efficient maintenance and dissemination of context information, but GLOSS

has been designed to manage location context only. To describe interests, consumers use adapters for each location type provided by a CMS. GLOSS uses the idea of HOME node.

3.4.4 Interoperability-Centered Work

CoCo [1] and Strang et al. [23] have proposed a different approach for interoperability among distributed CMS. They propose an abstract language and ontology that a CMS must use to publish context information in a common infrastructure. In this case, clients are not aware of CMS distribution, but access context from a centralized repository, i.e. a single CMS. The drawbacks of a unique access point to context are well-known: central point of failure and inefficient in distributed environments. Moreover, the maintenance of a central and general-purpose context model is unfeasible and the authors agree that describing a general purpose language for context interoperability is very challenging [2].

3.5 Bridging Approaches

Hesselman et al. [11, 12] have proposed a bridging mechanism among heterogeneous CMSs, enabling the creation of mappings between concepts of two different CMSs (Fig. 3.5), such as identity, query translation, context adaptation, and context reasoning. Using this approach to integrate CMSs, a context interest described according to one CMS's interface may include context information provided by any CMS that maintains a bridge with the aforementioned CMS. Although this approach enables interoperability among CMSs, it suffers from performance and scalability limitations, since each CMS represents a central point of access.

This approach presents other drawbacks:

- It inserts delays of context dissemination at each bridge;
- CMS still need to be properly distributed; and
- Bridges must be described for each space/pair of the required ubiquitous environment.

3.6 Summary

This chapter has discussed four middleware architectures for implementing distributed context management. To analyse how middleware systems support dynamic context-aware ecosystem, the chapter presented an analysis of how they support

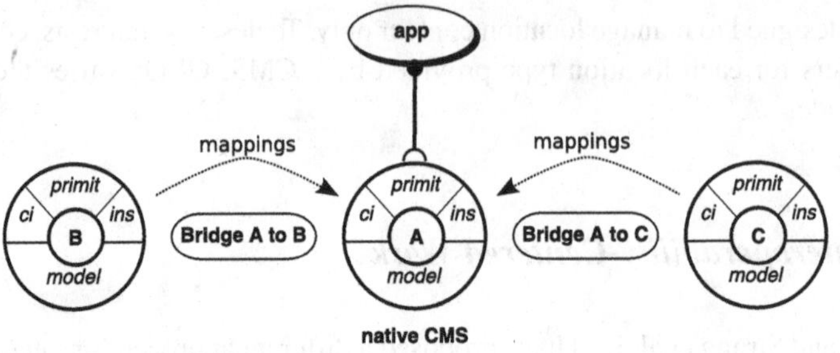

Fig. 3.5 Architecture of bridging approaches

context interest of variable wideness. As a conclusion of the chapter, there is no middleware system that support interest expression of types D_o, D_r, and D_c. In respect to the aspect of type coverage, some middleware systems support expressions T_a and T_s, since it depends on the context model adopted by the middleware. However, they do not support relationships among types defined in *different CMSs*. Hence, they hardly support an uniform description of context interests that could be applied and interpreted in the whole ecosystem. The next chapter presents an architecture and modeling approach that support the aforementioned context interests.

References

1. Buchholz, T., Krause, M., Linnhoff-Popien, C., Schiffers, M.: CoCo: dynamic composition of context information. In: First Annual International Conference on Mobile and Ubiquitous Systems: Networking and Services (MobiQuitous'04), pp. 335–343 (2004). doi: 10.1109/MOBIQ. 2004.1331740
2. Buchholz, T., Linnhoff-Popien, C.: Towards realizing global scalability in context-aware systems. LNCS: Location- and Context-Awareness, vol. 3479, pp. 26–39 (2005). doi:10.1007/ 11426646_4
3. Chen, G., Li, M., Kotz, D.: Design and implementation of a large-scale context fusion network. In: The First Annual International Conference on Mobile and Ubiquitous Systems: Networking and Services, Mobiquitous 2004. pp. 246–255 (2004). doi:10.1109/MOBIQ.2004.1331731
4. Dearle, A., Kirby, G.N.C., Morrison, R., McCarthy, A., Mullen, K., Yang, Y., Connor, R.C.H., Welen, P., Wilson, A.: Architectural support for global smart spaces. In: Proceedings of the 4th International Conference on Mobile Data Management MDM '03, pp. 153–164. Springer, London (2003)
5. Dey, A.K., Abowd, G.D., Salber, D.: A conceptual framework and a toolkit for supporting the rapid prototyping of context-aware applications. Hum. Comput. Interact. **16**(2–4), 97–166 (2001). doi:10.1207/S15327051HCI16234_02
6. Garlan, D., Siewiorek, D., Smailagic, A., Steenkiste, P.: Project aura: toward distraction-free pervasive computing. IEEE Pervasive Comput. **1**(2), 22–31 (2002). doi:10.1109/MPRV.2002.1012334
7. Grossmann, M., Bauer, M., Honle, N., Kappeler, U.P., Nicklas, D., Schwarz, T.: Efficiently managing context information for large-scale scenarios. In: Third IEEE International Conference

on Pervasive Computing and Communications, PerCom 2005, pp. 331–340 (2005). doi:10. 1109/PERCOM.2005.17

8. Henricksen, K., Indulska, J.: Developing context-aware pervasive computing applications: Models and approach. Pervasive Mob Comput **2**(1), 37–64 (2006). doi:10.1016/j.pmcj.2005. 07.003

9. Henricksen, K., Indulska, J., McFadden, T., Balasubramaniam, S.: Middleware for distributed context-aware systems. Lect Notes Comput Sci **3760**, 846–863 (2005)

10. Henricksen, K., Indulska, J., Rakotonirainy, A.: Modeling context information in pervasive computing systems. In: Proceedings of the First International Conference on Pervasive Computing, Pervasive '02, pp. 167–180. Springer, London (2002)

11. Hesselman, C., Benz, H., Pawar, P., Liu, F., Wegdam, M., Wibbles, M., Broens, T., Brok, J.: Bridging context management systems for different types of pervasive computing environments. In: First International Conference on Mobile Wireless Middleware, Operating Systems and Applications (MOBILWARE). ACM Press, Innsbruck, Austria (2008)

12. Hesselman, C., Eertink, H., Wibbels, M., Sheikh, K., Tokmakoff, A.: Controlled disclosure of context information across ubiquitous computing domains. In: IEEE International Conference on Sensor Networks, Ubiquitous and Trustworthy Computing SUTC '08. pp. 98–105 (2008). doi:10.1109/SUTC.2008.58

13. Hong, J.I., Landay, J.A.: An infrastructure approach to context-aware computing. Hum.-Comput. Interact. **16**(2–4), 287–303 (2001). doi:10.1207/S15327051HCI16234_11

14. Hong, J.I., Landay, J.A.: An architecture for privacy-sensitive ubiquitous computing. In: Proceedings of the 2nd International Conference on Mobile systems, Applications, and Services, MobiSys '04, pp. 177–189. ACM Press, New York (2004). doi:10.1145/990064. 990087

15. Judd, G., Steenkiste, P.: Providing contextual information to pervasive computing applications. In: Proceedings of the First IEEE International Conference on Pervasive Computing and Communications (PerCom 2003), pp. 133–142 (2003)

16. Kiani, S.L., Riaz, M., Lee, S., Lee, Y.K.: Context awareness in large scale ubiquitous environments with a service oriented distributed middleware approach. In: Proceedings of the Fourth Annual ACIS International Conference on Computer and Information Science (ICIS '05), pp. 513–518. IEEE Computer Society, Washington, DC (2005). doi:10.1109/ICIS.2005.40

17. Meneses, F.: Context management for heterogeneous administrative domains. In: Ferscha, A., et al. (eds.) Advances in pervasive computing, pp. 73–79. Austrian Computer Society, Vienna (2004)

18. Meneses, F.: Context management in ubiquitous systems. Ph.D. thesis, Escola de Engenharia, Universidade do Minho, Portugal (2007)

19. Riva, O.: Contory: A middleware for the provisioning of context information on smart phones. In: 7th International Middleware Conference ACM/IFIP/USENIX (Middleware'06). Melbourne (Australia) (2006)

20. Roman, M., Hess, C., Cerqueira, R., Ranganathan, A., Campbell, R., Nahrstedt, K.: A middleware infrastructure for active spaces. IEEE Pervasive Comput. **1**(4), 74–83 (2002). doi:10. 1109/MPRV.2002.1158281

21. Segall, B., Arnold, D., Boot, J., Henderson, M., Phelps, T.: Content Based Routing with Elvin4. In: Proceedings of AUUG2K, Canberra, June (2000)

22. Springer, T., Kadner, K., Steuer, F., Yin, M.: Middleware support for context-awareness in 4g environments. In: Proceedings of the International Symposium on on World of Wireless, Mobile and Multimedia Networks (WOWMOM '06), pp. 203–211. IEEE Computer Society, Washington, DC (2006). doi:10.1109/WOWMOM.2006.71

23. Strang, T., Linnhoff-Popien, C.: Service interoperability on context level in ubiquitous computing environments. In: Proceedings of International Conference an Advances in Infrastructure for Electronic Business, Education, Science, Medicine, and Mobile Technologies on the Internet. L'Aquila, Italy (2003)

24. van Kranenburg, H., Bargh, M., Iacob, S., Peddemors, A.: A context management framework for supporting context-aware distributed applications. IEEE Commun. Mag. **44**(8), 67–74 (Aug. 2006). doi:10.1109/MCOM.2006.1678112
25. Waldo, J.: The Jini architecture for network-centric computing. Commun. ACM **42**(7), 76–82 (1999). doi:10.1145/306549.306582

Chapter 4
Domain-Based Context Management

Abstract The support for context interests of variable wideness introduces several challenges for context management. First of all, consumers demand contextual inter-operability, in order to enable the interpretation of a context interest across various context management systems. In order to support expressions of closed and open domain, a middleware must support address resolution of context management systems and enable the definition of context scope boundaries and their management. Context management based on context domains is an approach for supporting interests of variable wideness in distributed and dynamic environments.

Keywords Context management · Context domains · Context scope · Context-aware computing · Distributed architectures

4.1 Introduction

The support for context interests of variable wideness introduces several challenges for context management. First of all, consumers demand contextual interoperability, in order to enable the interpretation of a context interest across various CMS. In order to support expressions of closed and open domain (D_c and D_o), a middleware must support address resolution of CMSs and enable the definition of context scope boundaries and their management.

This chapter presents the concept of *context domains* as an approach for enabling distributed context management and interests of variable wideness. Section 4.2 discusses requirements for enabling context interests of variable wideness. Section 4.3 presents the concept of *context domains*, and a primitive for describing context interests (Sect. 4.3.1). Finally, Sect. 4.4 presents a mechanism to deal with the complexity of managing context interest in a distributed architecture.

R. C. A. da Rocha and M. Endler, *Context Management for Distributed and Dynamic Context-Aware Computing*, SpringerBriefs in Computer Science, DOI: 10.1007/978-1-4471-4020-7_4, © The Author(s) 2012

4.2 Requirements

In order to support context interests of variable wideness, a context management approach must deal with expressions that may cover an unanticipated number of types and CMSs. On one hand, interests of abstract (T_a) and specific (T_s) type demand for contextual interoperability. On the other hand, the number of CMSs involved in open (D_o), relative (D_r), and closed (D_c) domain interests demands for the specification of boundaries of context scope.

To address these challenges and also scale with the number of consumers and providers, a context management approach must satisfy three main requirements: (i) provision of suitable primitives for describing context interests, (ii) implementation of an efficient mechanism for the interest delivery layer, and (iii) the support of an adequate context modeling approach.

4.2.1 Primitives for Describing Context Interests

Middleware for context-aware computing usually uses and adapts primitives for context interests from publish/subscribe systems. Although these primitives are suitable for centralized approaches, they do not allow consumers to determine which CMSs should process their interests, as required in distributed and dynamic environments. In particular, context interest for variable wideness demands for primitives to describe how broad or narrow an interest should be, in terms of CMS involved, as in expressions D_o, D_r and D_c.

4.2.2 Efficient Mechanisms for Interest Delivery Layer

Middleware for context management must implement an interest delivery layer that includes means of *dynamically* discovering: (i) the CMS that applies to a D_r expression, and (ii) the set of CMSs where a D_o expression has to be registered.

For example, the interest delivery layer should avoid broadcasting interest to all CMSs, because this would clearly hinder efficiency and scalability of the context management approach.

4.2.3 Adequate Context Modeling Approach

Context interests of variable wideness call for a context modeling approach that supports relationships among context types in different CMSs, as a means to support contextual interoperability. However, since the context models must be managed in a distributed environment, the modeling approach must be chosen properly so as to avoid management of huge context models (e.g. a single unified model for all CMSs) and to enable efficient context matching and dissemination.

In the proposed approach, contextual interoperability is based on super/subtyping relationships among context models of different CMSs. Moreover, the proposed approach enforces a strict overall decoupling of context management and context inference. In particular, the context modeling approach is data-oriented, i.e. it does not support model verification or reasoning, like in ontology-based approaches. Hence, context inference must be implemented externally to the CMS by an inference agent, instead of being described in a context model and controlled by CMS's model management. Instead, the proposed middleware adopts an object-oriented-based modeling approach, i.e. the CMS represents context instances as objects which have a type, a set of properties and corresponding values. Chapter 6 details the implementation of the modeling approach.

4.3 Context Domains

This book proposes context management based on the concept of *context domains*, as a means to organize hierarchically the context-aware ecosystem. A context domain establishes (i) the scope of a context model; (ii) the place and responsibility of the storage of context instances; (iii) the responsibility for managing context providers and consumers inside the domain; (iv) the management of remote and local context interests that involves locally stored context instances; and (v) a set of sub-domains. A context domain is an abstraction built on top of the traditional notion of network domain that establishes a context management scope.

Figure 4.1a shows an example of organization of context domains. The root domain (/) is the base domain on which all other domains are based. E and F are sub-domains of C, whereas C and D are sub-domains of B and /.

Each domain is responsible for managing the corresponding context model depicted in Fig. 4.1b. Context models distributed across domains establish a hierarchical relationship among their context types. The super- and sub-domains establish a relationship of containment, whereas context models of super/subdomains establish a relationship of super/subtyping. Context types of a domain may be modeled as subtypes of context types of any super-domain: a context type defined in a model M_N may inherit from any type T from M_J, if N is a sub-domain of J. For example, consider that M_I, M_B, M_C, M_E and M_F are context models of the domains root (/), B, C, E and F, respectively, as depicted in Fig. 4.1b. Then, a context type described in M_E or M_F may be modeled as a subtype of a type modeled either in M_C, M_B or M_I. Hence, context domains also establish a domain-distributed hierarchy of types.

To represent a context domain, this book adopts the following syntactic structure: a concatenation of names separated by ".", from the more, to the less specific domain and use of lowercase characters, as in Internet domain names. For example, the domain G of the Fig. 4.1a is represented by the string g.d.b.

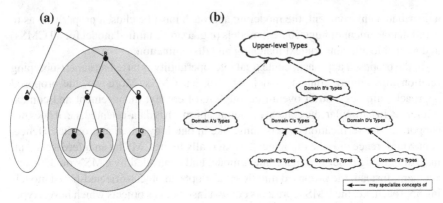

Fig. 4.1 Example of distributed CMSs organized in context domains. **a** Domain organization; **b** Corresponding hierarchy of context domains

4.3.1 Description of Context Interests

In a domain-based context-aware ecosystem, each context instance is stored in a specific domain and is associated to a certain context type in the distributed type tree. An instance belongs to the domain where its provider has published it. A context instance $i_{d'}^{t'}$, where d' is a domain and t' is a type, satisfies an interest $I_{d_j}^{t_i}$ where d_j is a domain and t_i is a context type, if t' is a sub-type of t_i and d' is a sub-domain of d_j. Type is a mandatory parameter of an interest, whereas a domain parameter may be used or not according to consumer's needs.

The description of a context interest adopts the following structure:

```
<type>(<entity-id>)[@<instance-domain-constraint>]
     [where <attribute-constraints>]
```

where

`<type>` is the context type.
`<entity-id>` is a domain-based identifier of the entity
`<instance-domain-constraint>` is a domain name, which constrains the domains where the context instances for this interest will be searched.
`<attribute-constraints>` is a set of constraints that specify the condition, in terms of attribute values of a type `<type>`, that satisfies the interest.

For example, the interest `Device(device01)@c.b where (Battery-Level < 60)`, where `Device` is a context type modeled on the root domain and the interest is applied in the same domain tree of Fig. 4.1. A context instance satisfies this interest if all the following conditions are true:

- The type of the instance is `Device` or any of its sub-types.
- The instance is describing the entity `device01`.

- The context instance is published at the domain c.b or any of its sub-domains e.c.b or f.c.b.
- The instance's attribute BatteryLevel has a value that is less than 60. BatteryLevel is an attribute of type Device.

In this example, the global contextual interoperability is guaranteed, since Device is modeled at the root domain and thus it is already recognized at any existing domain.

In a context interest, the predefined domain @current may be used for <instance-domain-constraint> to specify the domain where the interested consumer is currently active. An expression with @current(Location(i)) represents the current domain of entity i. In both cases, the concrete domain associated to @current may change dynamically.

The proposed primitive enables the specification of all types of context interest discussed in Chap. 2. Depending on the <instance-domain-constraint>, an application may define an expression with a different coverage of domains, i.e. an expression uses a more narrow domain, when the domain described in <instance-domain-constraint> is more specific. If there is no <instance-domain-constraint>, then the expression is for an entirely open domain, i.e., any domain may potentially contain context instances that satisfy the interest. If an expression contains @current, then it describes an interest of relative domain (D_r).

The type coverage of an expression depends on the <type> parameter: e.g. a more specific type represents a T_s expression, whereas a more general type represents a T_a expression, which could be a root level type in the more abstract case.

4.4 Managing Context Interests Through Domain-Addressable Entities

The complexity of managing a context interest depends on the number of domains w involved in its resolution, i.e. the domains that must execute the context matching function against the interest. An interest must be registered in each of these domains. This book will use the term *wideness* of an interest for the number w.

The value of w may range from 1 to the total number of domains of an ecosystem. As shown in Fig. 4.2, an interest selects a part of a domain tree, and w represents its complexity.

Let $I_{d_j}^{t_i}$ be an interest for the context type i, and restricted to the domain j. The wideness w of the interest depends on t_i and d_j. d_j restricts the interest for the domain j and their subdomains. The wideness may depend on t_i if i is defined in a subdomain of j. If i is defined in j or one of its super-domains, then it does not interfere in the wideness of the interest. In the example shown in Fig. 4.1, an interest $I_{d_C}^{t_B}$ restricts the interest processing to the domain C and their subdomains (E and F), because C is a more restricted domain of B. However, for an interest $I_{d_j}^{t_G}$, the type will be

Fig. 4.2 Interest selecting a part of the domain tree

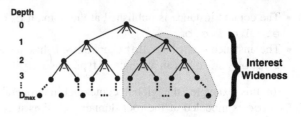

determinant in the restriction of domains that will process the interest, since G is a more specific domain than $/$.

The implementation of a context selection (see Sect. 2.2.5) through distributed domains is more challenging, because the context resolution may not be localized in a single and statically known domain. In the worst case, if an interest uses a root level type and does not have a further restriction to a more specific domain, any node may contain context instances that satisfy the interest. In general, the number of nodes grows exponentially with the wideness of a context interest.

In order to minimize the overhead of the distributed context selection function, an entity will be localized in a domain specified by its `<entity-id>`. For example, a student of the Department of Informatics of PUC-Rio called Alice, could be identified by the id `alice@inf.puc-rio.br`. As a result, domain `inf.puc-rio.br` is also responsible for maintaining the user `alice`, which is Alice's *home domain*. A home domain maintains references to all domains that contain instances that describe their entities. For example, if a provider at `gcontext.google.com` starts publishing context instances of `Location` type for the entity `alice@inf.puc-rio.br`, then the domain responsible for `inf.puc-rio.br` will have registered that `gcontext.google.com` is maintaining the aforementioned context instance. However, it is clear that there must be an inter-domain protocol to maintain consistently such references. For example, these references must be always updated whenever another domain starts maintaining instances of a domain's entity. Section 6.3.3 discusses the implementation of this inter-domain protocol.

When a consumer registers an interest, the home domain of the corresponding entity is queried about the domains that contain the instances that satisfy the context interest. Then, the interest is registered at each of these domains. Since the domains that keep entity's context may change dynamically, the home domain must be kept updated of the domains that contain registries for each consumer's interests. As a result, each domain can implement the context selection function for interests that involve its home entities, returning only domain names that satisfy an interest. This approach avoids registering an interest in all the set of domains defined by the interest's wideness w. Chapter 6 discusses in more details how a home domain works.

4.5 Summary

This chapter has presented a middleware approach for supporting distributed context management and distributed context modeling, in order to support context interests of variable wideness. In addition, the proposed approach is complemented with a primitive for describing context interests that eases that management of interests in distributed CMSs and, at the same time, avoids the development of complex interest expressions to describe an application adaptation. The next chapter shows a example scenario of using the proposed primitive to describe a context-aware application, whose interests depend on the application's current domain and may change at runtime. The scenario demonstrates the utility of the proposed primitive.

Chapter 5
Usage Scenario

Abstract In distributed and dynamic context-aware environments, applications need to specify context interests of variable wideness. This chapter presents a scenario for a context-aware application in a distributed environment which considers migration cross networks, context domains, heterogeneity, and interaction with various context providers. The scenario demonstrates aspects of actual ubiquitous applications, such as interoperation across diverse environents of context-aware computing. The application is a location-aware messaging application, and it is applied to a tourist scenario.

Keywords Context management · Tourist application · Map-based application · Distributed architectures

5.1 Introduction

This chapter describes a context-aware messaging application and a usage scenario that make use of the interest expressions proposed in Chap. 2. In this scenario, a tourist uses a location-aware application to plan an itinerary in a city, which involves roaming through different context domains. Section 5.2 presents the application adopted in the scenario, which is based on the *UMessenger 2.0* example, described in Chap. 2. Section 5.3 presents a scenario of the application usage by a tourist in the city of Rio de Janeiro. The scenario considers the context-aware infrastructure (i.e. context domains, providers and models) described in Sect. 5.4. Section 5.5 presents the context interests required for the application. Finally, Sect. 5.6 discusses the benefits of using context interests in the proposed scenario, based on the concept of domains, in terms of an optimized number of overall notifications sent to the application.

R. C. A. da Rocha and M. Endler, *Context Management for Distributed and Dynamic*   49
Context-Aware Computing, SpringerBriefs in Computer Science,
DOI: 10.1007/978-1-4471-4020-7_5, © The Author(s) 2012

5.2 Application Description

Consider an application based on *UMessenger 2.0*, as described in Chap. 2, developed for a context-aware infrastructure based on the concept of context domains. The application would be able to:

1. Retrieve a global map that describes physical areas and place objects in the map through its geographic coordinates (i.e. latitude, longitude, altitude). This map corresponds to a broader map, i.e. any other map can be described as a part of this map and, thus, any object can be placed on it. The application assumes that there is a static and well-known provider of this map.
2. Retrieve a specific map for a physical area, e.g. a building or a public park. For a certain place, there may exist more than one service that provides such a specific map, but the application will only retrieve the map provided on the more specific domain.
3. Display the current location of a user, on either the global or a specific map.
4. Display the location of user's buddies, also either on a global or a map specific to buddy's current locations.
5. Display nearest reference objects in a map. These objects can have particular semantics: e.g. a printer in an office or a tourist attraction in a tourist map. However, the application does not interpret such semantics and only shows them in the map with the corresponding descriptive information.

Each of these application's features represents a context information of which the application wants to be notified and, thus, translates into application's context interest. The idea of map's scope is clearly implemented through context domains.

5.3 Usage Scenario

Consider that a tourist wants to explore on his own the city of Rio de Janeiro. He is part of a tourist group, which he wants to temporarily leave at the hotel and to use the *UMessenger 2.0* to:

- obtain location information of tourist places and points of interest.
- synchronize his route with the activities (or schedule) of the group.
- obtain more detailed information about the places he visits.

He plans to leave the hotel to visit the Museu Nacional de Belas Artes (*Museum of Fine Arts* - MNBA), and then visit Santa Teresa district, through a tourist tram (called "bondinho"), to attend the artistic event "Santa Teresa de Portas Abertas". He plans to rejoin the group at the end of the trip, or when he realises that the group is attending an interesting event.

For this scenario, consider that the city is fully covered by a context-aware infrastructure based on the concept of domains, and that satisfies the following requirements:

Table 5.1 User interaction storyline

Place	Actions
Hotel	• User wants to go to another tourist place
	• Checks if his friends are on-line
	• Leaves a message to some group members (and the guide of the group)
	• Check directions to the Museum of Fine Arts and then to the Santa Teresa district
	• Takes a taxi
Street	• Checks directions to the next destination and compare to taxi route
	• Arrives at the museum
Museum	• Checks maps of the Museum
	• Chooses a direction to start the visit
	• Checks : current location, suggestions and descriptions
	• Checks directions to Santa Teresa (user explicitly switches to global map)
	• Starts walking to the tram station.
Santa Teresa	• Checks the schedule of the tram.
	• Queries buddies' activity
	• Searches for map directions to specific artist studios.
	• Switches to the geomap and searches for restaurants
	• Searches the current location of the group
	• Tries to contact the group's tourist guide (unavailable for voice, text messages)
	• Initiates a conversation with a friend
	• Checks directions to Copacabana district
Copacabana	• Rejoins his buddies.

- There is network connectivity in all places that are part of the scenario, through either WiFi-based networks or a cellular network.
- Hotel, MNBA, the tram and Santa Teresa provide specific maps that describe them. For example, the tram's map describes its route. Moreover, MNBA and the hotel have their own location mechanisms to locate users on their maps.
- MNBA, hotel and Santa Teresa provide, on the map, points of interest such as, respectively, art objects (e.g. sculptures, paintings), facilities and artist's studios. Each point has descriptive information, e.g. paintings provide additional information such as related media, history of the painting and comments by experts.

Consider as an example of the user's actions, the storyline described in Table 5.1.

5.4 Context-Aware Infrastructure

This section describes the context-aware infrastructure—domains, models and providers—that is the framework upon which application's context interests are formulated.

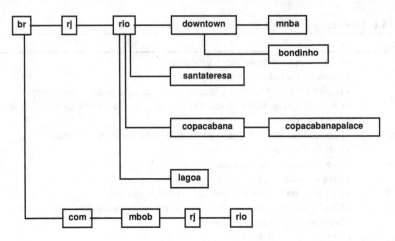

Fig. 5.1 Domains adopted on the scenario

5.4.1 Context Domains

Figure 5.1 depicts the relevant context domains adopted for the scenario. The branch `mbob.com.br` corresponds to the domain related to the cellular network infrastructure of a mobile network operator (*MBob*), where all of its subdomains are also managed by this operator. The branch `rio.rj.br` contains domains that correspond to a physical scope of the city of Rio de Janeiro. This branch includes subdomains that represent the city's districts (e.g. Downtown, Santa Teresa).

Figure 5.2 shows the association of these domains with specific geographic areas in the city.

5.4.2 Context Models and Providers

The modeling of the scenario uses context types that enable the description of location and maps. Figure 5.3 shows a simple context model adopted for the scenario. This modeling considers that a geosymbolic location contains both a symbolic location and its respective geographic coordinates. For example, if `MNBABuilding` is a geosymbolic location, than this type also encapsulates the corresponding geographic coordinates of the building. This mapping from symbolic location to geographic location is important to enable a visualization of symbolic locations in a geographic map. In the scenario, interests for location must be based on the abstract `GeoLocation`, instead of `Location`, because the application needs to place any object in a geographic map. A similar rationale applies to the hierarchy of types that inherits from `Map`.

Figure 5.4 shows a simplified diagram of entities adopted in the scenario.

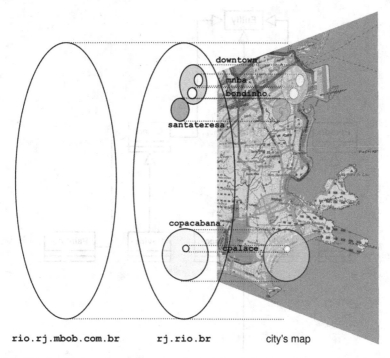

Fig. 5.2 Relationship between context domains and the city's geographic areas, in the scenario © OpenStreeMap contributors, CC BY-SA

Fig. 5.3 Context types

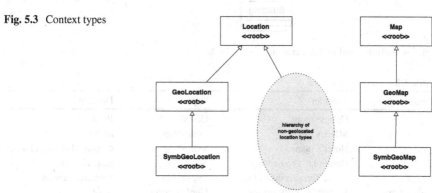

Table 5.2 shows the context providers of the scenario and the corresponding context types that they publish.

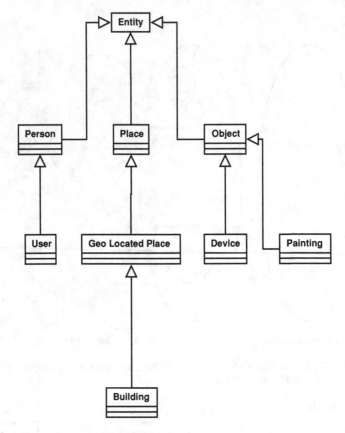

Fig. 5.4 Entities used in the scenario

Table 5.2 Context providers

Abstract type	Provider	Type	Domain
Map	Google maps	GeoMap	Root
	MNBA maps	SymbMap	MNBA
	Hotel's maps	SymbMap	Copacabanapalace
	Bondinho's route map	SymbMap	Bondinho
	Santa Teresa's event map	SymbMap	Santateresa
Location	Embedded GPS sensor	GeoLocation	Root
	MNBA location system	SymbLocation	MNBA
	Hotel's location system	SymbLocation	Copacabanapalace

5.5 Implementation of Application's Context Interests

Application's context interests must describe the consumption of the context described in Sect. 5.2. There are two main context types the application is interested in: Location and Map. For the following examples, consider that the identifier of user's device is alice-device, which has inf.puc-rio.br as a home domain. Then, the application registers the following interests:

- GeoLocation(alice-device@inf.puc-rio.br) describes an interest for receiving the location of the device, which may be provided by any context provider.
- GeoLocation(alice-device@inf.puc-rio.br)@current describes an interest for receiving the location of the device according to a GeoLocation's context provider in the current domain of the device.
- GeoMap(myCurrentLoc)@gcontext.google.com where (zoom Factor = 8) describes an interest to receive a GeoMap, provided by the domain gcontext.google.com and that must satisfy the constraint (zoomFactor < 8). In this example, zoomFactor is an attribute that allows to restrict the coverage of the map that a consumer receives.
- GeoMap@current describes an interest to receive the map provided by the current user's domain, which is the most specific map for the user's location.
- Object@current where (distance(mylocation) <50m) describes an interest to receive any object, provided by the current domain, whose distance to the location of user's device is less than 50 m. This example considers that distance is a constraint operator for the context type Object.

5.6 Analysis of Interest Dissemination

Figure 5.5 shows a diagram of domain switches of the application, according to the storyline previously presented in Table 5.1. For the sake of simplicity, consider SMap, GMap, GLoc, and SLoc the context types SymbGeoMap, GeoMap, GeoLocation, and SymbGeoLocation, respectively.

When the user wants to check directions to Downtown and Santa Teresa, he configures the application to switch from domain rio.copacabana. copacabanapalace to rio, because he needs to use a map that describes the city, instead of the hotel. At each switch, a former interest may be unregistered, which depends on application policy. For example, the application's policy could establish that if the user does not switch back to the current domain within a given interval than the application will unregister the respective interest.

When the user roams through domains 2 to 4, the application receives notifications of map and location from the provider at the root domain, because there is no more specific provider for either of the context types. When the domain switches to rio.downtown.mnba at 5, the application starts receiving notifications about

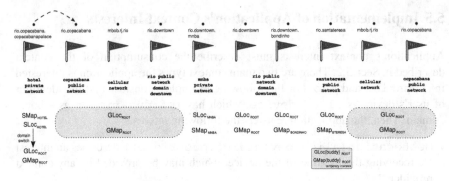

Fig. 5.5 Context domain switches

maps and device's location according to providers at the MNBA. When the user exits the museum (at 6), a new domain change occurs for the broader domain `rio.downtown`. The application continues in this domain until the user gets close to the tram station (at 7), where the application switches again to the domain `rio.downtown.bondinho`, and starts receiving notification about maps provided in `rio.downtown.bondinho`, i.e. `SymGeoMap` of domain `bondinho`, although it continues to receive notifications of `GeoLocation`. When the user arrives at Santa Teresa (at 9), the application's context domain changes again for `rio.downtown.santateresa`. As a result, the application starts receiving notification for maps provided in `rio.downtown.santateresa`, which describes artist's studios and event locations. Then, the user checks the group location, using as a reference the location of one of his/her buddies. To display buddy's location, the application has to register the following interest:

`Location(buddy-device-id)@current(buddy-device-id)`

This expression describes an interest for the location of the buddy according to *his* most specific location provider. The expression's interest is temporary: as soon as the user is satisfied with the buddy's location, he stops tracking buddy's location and the corresponding interest is unregistered.

As shown in the diagram, the usage of the primitives for describing interests decreases the number of notifications a consumer receives. In particular, context of types `GeoMap` and `GLoc` are always available for the application. In domains that these context types are not relevant, the application does not receive notifications. In a scenario where there is a large number of location providers, these additional notifications could decrease the performance of the application and the middleware.

5.7 Summary

This chapter has shown a distributed scenario for a messenger application that adapts its behavior according to the current user's domain. Sections 5.5 and 5.6 have shown, respectively, the implementation of the scenario using the primitives proposed in the previous chapter and an analysis of context dissemination in the scenario's domains. These sections have shown that the proposed approach enables the development of complex context-aware application and efficient dissemination of context. The next chapter presents the design of a middleware that implements the proposed approach.

Chapter 6
Middleware for Context Management Based on Context Domains

Abstract Context management based on context domains is an approach for supporting interests of variable wideness in distributed and dynamic environments. Context domains establish distributed boundaries for both context modeling and management. The design of a distributed middleware based on this concept should address an architecture that enables efficient context-based interaction in both localized and distributed pairs of consumer–provider, protocols for discovering context management systems, and a suitable programming model for context-aware applications. In addition, the middleware should address some additional requirements, such as its usage in resource-constrained portable devices.

Keywords Context management · Middleware · Context-aware computing · Open distributed systems · Distributed architectures

6.1 Introduction

Chapter 4 presented an approach for context management that supports context interests of variable wideness. To demonstrate the feasibility of the proposed approach, this chapter presents a distributed middleware that implements the concept of context domains. In addition, the design of the middleware addresses some additional requirements, such as its usage in resource-constrained portable devices.

This chapter is organized as follows. Section 6.2 presents the design rationale that drove the implementation of the middleware and the main assumptions adopted in design time. Section 6.3 presents the middleware architecture, services and protocols. Section 6.4 presents the cNode: a middleware instance that runs on each client device. Section 6.5 presents the context modeling approach and the mechanism for deploying new context types in the distributed architecture. Finally, Sect. 6.6 presents the programming model for context consumers and providers.

R. C. A. da Rocha and M. Endler, *Context Management for Distributed and Dynamic Context-Aware Computing*, SpringerBriefs in Computer Science, DOI: 10.1007/978-1-4471-4020-7_6, © The Author(s) 2012

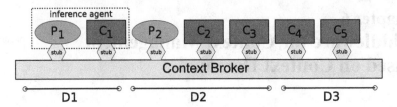

Fig. 6.1 Context broker

6.2 Design Rationale

To enable seamless evolution of context types, the proposed middleware architecture makes use of stubs for each context type that embedded the code required for accessing and managing instances of the corresponding context type. These stubs are automatically generated from a XML-based specification of a context type (see Sect. 6.5). The underlying code is responsible for handling changes in the actual context type and context domain that the application is dealing with. From the perspective of applications, context access is strongly typed: i.e. the type of a context information, in terms of the corresponding language mapping, is defined at development time, so as applications can be statically prepared to recognize the type of a context information.

Context subtyping is implemented as inheritance on the object-oriented paradigm. The translation of context types/instances to classes/objects accordingly to object-oriented paradigm, enable the use of polymorphism mechanism, thus allowing applications to access context instances without requiring them to previously determine which is the actual type they are referencing. This mechanism provides a natural way to handle both *abstract* (T_s) and *specific* (T_a) type expressions at programming level.

The middleware provides transparency of CMS address resolution through services for automatic self-discovery of domain membership and inter-domain hand-off management of context consumers and providers. In order to dynamically discover which domains contains context instances satisfying a context interest, the middleware implements the mechanism previously described in Sect. 4.4.

Essentially, there are three components that interact to create, disseminate and use context information: context providers, context consumers and the Context Broker, as shown in Fig. 6.1. The Context Broker is an abstraction for the distributed domain management services, provided by a network of context management nodes (Sect. 6.3). Each context management node is responsible for a context domain.

As an orthogonal requirement, the middleware must be able to run in resource-constrained devices, such as PDAs and smartphones. To enable efficient interactions in a distributed scenario, the middleware adopts a dual mode of context management. On one hand, context published locally to a device, is also stored locally, avoiding network communication for interactions between a consumer and a provider that run on the same device. On the other hand, if the context published by a provider needs

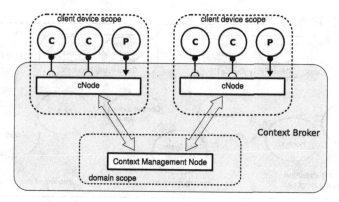

Fig. 6.2 Component interaction

to be shared with remote consumers (i.e. external to the device), then the middleware stores it on the infrastructured network , at context management nodes.

6.3 Architecture and Services

As mentioned before, the Context Broker is an abstraction of a network of distributed context management nodes (CMN). A CMN implements a context management system responsible for a particular domain, thus intermediating any interaction among consumers and providers of a domain. As shown in Fig. 6.2, each client device runs a cNode, an entity that is responsible for implementing distribution transparency of context access, to deal with local context-aware interactions (i.e. device-local providers and consumers) and context access in disconnected mode.

A context domain is implemented as an IP-based network domain, such that the context domain of a consumer corresponds to the domain defined by its current point of network attachment.

A context management node is composed of the four tiers shown in Fig. 6.3:

- *management tier*, responsible for implementing context management
- *proxy tier*, responsible for maintaining proxies of context consumers and providers.
- *distributed domain tier*, responsible for domain management tasks, such as domain naming and inter-domain hand-off.
- *context distribution and entity management tier*, responsible for the management of entities registered in a domain, resolving which CMNs a specific context interest must be registered.

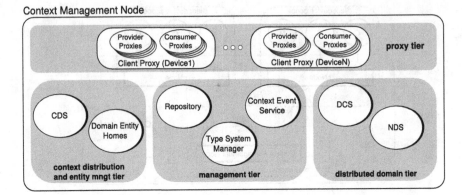

Fig. 6.3 Middleware services

Fig. 6.4 Management tier
protocol interaction

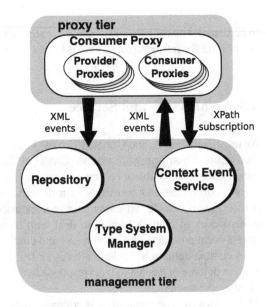

6.3.1 Management Tier

The *management tier* aggregates services that are responsible for context management, i.e. storage of context information and management of context interests. Context providers and consumers interact with the management tier indirectly through their corresponding proxies, maintained by the *proxy tier*. Hence, the management tier only interacts with CMN-local proxies, and does not need to be aware of mobility or distribution of clients. The management tier provides three services: the Context Event Service, the Context Repository and the Type System Manager.

6.3.1.1 Context Repository

The Context Repository maintains a XML database that stores context information, enabling processing of synchronous queries from consumers. The repository also stores the representation of context types, i.e. the context model, which is used by the *Type System Manager* (management tier) to control model changes.

6.3.1.2 Context Event Service

The *Context Event Service* (CES) is responsible for asynchronous delivery of contextual events to clients that have previously registered context interests. CES stores contextual events (i.e. changes of context data) and executes the matching function to evaluate if an event satisfies any context interests registered locally.

Context is published as an XML event and interest are registered as XPath subscriptions as shown in Fig. 6.4. This approach provides flexibility for constructing interest and generating stubs, even if the context type evolves.

CES is implemented on the basis of Naradabrokering [2], a distributed publish/subscribe system. The middleware uses a underlying network of Naradabrokering nodes to disseminate efficiently[1] context events in a distributed network of management nodes.

6.3.1.3 Type System Manager

The *Type System Manager* (TSM) is responsible for maintaining the context model for a domain and for controlling the type deployment mechanism (see Sect. 6.5). Context types are stored in an XML repository using the XML notation described in Sect. 6.5.1.

When a new context consumer/provider is deployed, stubs are generated in development time from the current XML description obtained from TSM. The TSM maintains a local database with copies of context types defined in its superdomains. To avoid maintaining a large model database, the TSM copies supertypes on-demand, i.e. only at deployment of a new context type, or when a new interest is registered.

The following changes in the context model may introduce inconsistencies in type system management:

- change or removal of a type attribute
- change of a type name
- hierarchy change, such as a removal of a type

When deploying such changes, the domain administrator is warned that a change introduces type system inconsistencies, which may invalidate interests based on the

---

[1] In terms of routing events to a group of consumers in a distributed network.

former version of the type. Any other change keeps the context models structurally consistent.

The usage of XML for describing context instances and types enables a loosely-coupled mapping between stubs that interact with the middleware and the actual context type definition. As a concrete benefit, if a change is structurally consistent, both consumers and providers may use outdated versions of stubs for a context type, without requiring the redevelopment or restarting of an application.

TSM adopts a lazy approach for type change propagation: a change in one type is propagated to its subdomains on-demand, i.e. in the development of consumer/provider that uses the type.

6.3.2 Proxy Tier

The proxy tier is responsible for maintaining proxies that represent all context consumers and providers of a domain. When a device enters a domain, a corresponding client proxy is created. A client proxy aggregates all the consumers and providers running at a client device, as depicted in Fig. 6.3. Each consumer proxy corresponds to a context interest created by applications at this client device. When an interest is unregistered, the proxy tier removes the corresponding consumer proxy. A consumer proxy may also maintain an interest for context in another domain. When a client device roams to another domain, the proxy tier transfers the corresponding client proxy to the new domain, as a part of the inter-domain hand-off protocol. Hence, the proxy tier is responsible for the mobility management of client devices.

A consumer proxy maintains context interests and primarily receives notifications for an interest match. A consumer proxy forwards any interest match to the actual consumer running at the client device.

Each client device has a unique identifier composed of a `device id` (currently, its MAC address) and a domain name where the device must be previously registered. A client device is modeled and managed as an entity of type `Device`. For each client device in a domain, the CMN maintains an instance of `NetworkConnectivity` context which maps a device to its current IP address, besides other network connectivity attributes. The proxy tier uses `NetworkConnectivity` context to manage the device's mobility.

The communication between proxies and a client device is implemented by a lightweight connectionless protocol based on UDP. This protocol uses leases to maintain the device's connectivity state, such that the proxy can stop forwarding notifications when the device becomes disconnected or connected to another network.

Table 6.1 Example of Entity Home entry for an entity **e**

	Type	Hosting domains	Client proxies
1	B	d_1, d_2, d_3	p_1, p_2
2	C	d_2, d_4	p_3
3	D	d_2, d_5	p_3

A is supertype of B and C

6.3.3 Context Distribution and Entity Management Tier

Context Distribution and Entity Management Tier is responsible for managing entities registered at a domain and to register the domains that contain context instances of each registered entity. The goal of this tier is to implement a mechanism for discovering which CMN contains context instances that may satisfy an interest, avoiding the need to broadcast interest registrations to all CMNs. This tier implements the concept of Entity Home and the mechanism of resolving context interest described in Sect. 4.4

6.3.3.1 Entity Home

Entity Home is a repository of entities that belong to a domain and that maintains updated references to both domains and proxies that have registered some interests for an entity. For each entity **e**, the Entity Home maintains several entries with three attributes

- **Type**: a context type **T**, associated with the entity **e**,
- **Hosting Domains**: set of domains that maintain context instances of type **T** for the entity **e**,
- **Client proxies**: references to client proxies that maintain interests for the context type **T** for the entity **e**. This attribute may be empty if there is no registered proxy for **e**.

Table 6.1 shows an example of an entity home table, where both B and C are subtypes of A (not shown) and D has not relationship with A, B or C. Any new consumer or provider for a context that describes **e**, causes changes on entries of the Entity Home table.

If a provider starts publishing context that describes *e* of type C at the domain d_4, the Entity Home inserts d_4 at the column "Hosting Domains". If a consumer register an interest for any context type of *e*, then the Entity Home includes the corresponding client proxy reference for the type that satisfies the interest. At the registry of each domain, Entity Home returns the respective proxies in the table. At the registry of each client proxy, the Entity Home returns the referencing domains for types satisfying the interest.

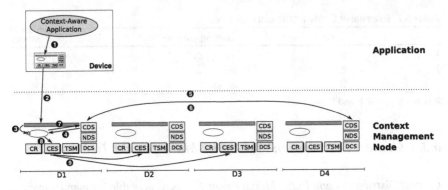

Fig. 6.5 Interaction among distributed domains to register and to update a context interest

For the same example, the registry of a new consumer's interest will produce the following changes on the Entity Home table:

- $B(e)$: returns the hosting domains d_1, d_2 and d_3, and registers the corresponding proxy at line 1.
- $B(e)@d_3$: the same of the previous interest, but returns only d_3.
- $A(e)$: returns domains d_1 to d_4, inserts a new entry for A and registers the corresponding proxy. The hosting domain will be empty.
- $A(e)@d_4$: returns d_4 and register the proxy at 2.
- $D(e)@d_1$: returns a empty set of domains, since there is no d_1 or subdomain of d_1 at line 3, and register the proxy at line 3.

6.3.3.2 Context Distribution Service and Interest Registration

The *Context Distribution Service* is responsible for maintaining the Entity Homes, which verifies if there are domains with context instances that may satisfy a context interest and to trigger its registration on the respective domain.

Consider an entity $a@D_4$, registered in domain D_4, and that both D_2 and D_3 maintain context instances for this entity. Figure 6.5 shows the sequence of interactions among each instance of the middleware service, running in different domains, when a consumer registers a context interest I_a for $a@D_4$. For the sake of simplicity, consider that I_a refers to the same context type of the instances maintained in D_2 and D_3. At the moment of I_a registration, the distributed service will interact as follows:

1. Application registers its context interest (I_a) at the local cNode.
2. cNode sends the context interest to the CMN of the current domain D_1.
3. D_1's CMN creates a consumer proxy for I_a, say p_{I_a}
4. p_{I_a} sends its request to CDS_{D_1}
5. CDS_{D_1} requests to CDS_{D_4} the domains with instances that may satisfy I_a, informing the context type and the entity ($a@D_4$) of I_a, as well the proxy p_{I_a}.

6. After checking the Entity Home of $a @ D_4$, CDS_{D_4} sends to CDS_{D_1} the domains D_2 and D_3. CDS_{D_4} includes a reference to p_{I_a} in the Entity Home.
7. Then, CES_{D_1} sends to the proxy p_{I_a} the request for notifications for such events, in the respective domains, and p_{I_a} updates the ids of the notification it may receive.
8. p_{I_a} request CES_{D_1} to register its two interests (for D_2 and D_3).
9. CES_{D_1} propagates the interest registration to CES_{D_2} and CES_{D_3}.

6.3.4 Distributed Domain Tier

The distributed domain tier is responsible for domain-specific tasks such as discovery, inter-domain hand-off dispatch and domain naming. This tier contains two services: node discovery and domain configuration service.

6.3.4.1 Node Discovery Service

The *Node Discovery Service* (NDS) is responsible for discovering and advertising the network's context domain. NDS sends advertisements to its local network, so that clients are able to detect a domain change through domain announcements. NDS uses the Service Location Protocol [1] (SLP) as the lower-level service discovery mechanism.

For example, when a client device is turned on, the middleware discovers a CMN service responsible for the current network and defines the device's home domain, that registers the client device's proxy. If there is no CMN in the network, then the middleware contacts the device's home domain, identified by its device id. This is the only case where the proxy is registered in a CMN of another network.

When a client device connects to another network, the protocol executes the following actions:

1. The device recognizes a new domain through NDS domain announcements.
2. The device sends a hand-off procedure request, informing its domain.
3. NDS triggers the hand-off procedure, which transfers the client proxy from the previous CMN to the current domain's CMN.

NDS publishes a domain in SLP, adopting the service name ucms, so as the service URI is service:ucms://<ip-address>:<port>. Currently, the service registry in SLP contains only one attribute: the domain name.

6.3.4.2 Domain Configuration Service

The *Domain Configuration Service* (DCS) is a complementary service for a CMN responsible for mapping domain names to IP network addresses, which a CMN needs

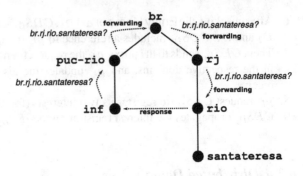

Fig. 6.6 Solving the address of the domain `br.rj.rio.santateresa`

to interact to another CMN. At domain deployment time, DCS registers a sub-domain at its super domain, and then each domain maintains references for its subdomains. Resolution of the domain address is based on the domain tree, as shown in Fig. 6.6. This figure illustrates how the DCS responsible for the domain `br.puc-rio.inf` resolves the name of domain `br.rj.rio.santateresa`.

6.4 Client Node

The client node cNode implements the basic mechanisms of the management tier but restricted to scope of a device: it manages locally restricted interests, implements transparent access of CMN, and handles device disconnection. The cNode intercepts all requests - from both consumers or providers -, and forwards them to the domain node, when necessary.

The cNode stores all locally published context, i.e. whose provider is local to the device. The middleware uses an opportunistic approach for publishing context remotely, waiting to piggybacking a publishing on the next network communication. A local context is published also in the home domain node of the device.

For efficiency reasons, both the context repository and the event service are based on a relational database, instead of a XML database. At the device local scope, there is no support for evolution: if the internal context model changes, then an application that uses it may need to be restarted. This policy is suitable because, in the scope of a device, the same user is responsible for managing both applications and context changes.

6.5 Modeling and Deployment of Context Types

As shown in Fig. 6.1, both context providers and consumers interact with the Context Broker through context type *stubs*. They encapsulate the underlying code required to request or publish a specific instance of a context type, and type dependencies (e.g.

supertypes, entity types). The developer of a context-aware application includes the stubs of the required context types, which map a context type to object-oriented language constructions. From the perspective of an application developer, the access to context information is strongly typed, since the application accesses classes that have a 1:1 mapping to context types.

The deployment of a context type, which involves two main steps: context modeling and the context model processing. The first step consists of modeling the new context information using an XML-based description called DCMML (Distributed Context Modeling Markup Language). In a DCMML file, the context modeler[2] specifies attributes, characteristics and relationships with previously specified context.

In the context model processing step, a *Context Tool* reads the DCMML file and executes the following tasks:

1. Validates the DCMML syntax and the context model, interacting with the TSM of the domain where the type is being deployed;
2. Updates the context type system and initializes the repository for storing the new context information;
3. Generates a library containing the language bindings for describing interests and accessing the deployed context.

Section 7.2 describes how the context tool implements the language bindings for Java VM and Dalvik VM (Android platform). Context Tool alerts the user about the consequences of the changes in deployment.

6.5.1 Context Modeling and Representation

Each DCMML modeling file models a unique context type, and contains the following elements:

- `Context Type:Domain` - a name that describes the context type and the domain where the type will be deployed.
- `Supertype:Domain` - the context supertype and the domain where the supertype is modeled. Both supertype and supertype's domain must be consistent with the domain of the type: the domain of the supertype must be either the same or a superdomain of the type domain.
- `Entity` - the entity type that the context decribes.
- `(attribute,type)` * - a set of attribute names and the corresponding attribute types.

The listing below shows an example of a DCMML document that describes a context type `DeviceContext`, modeled in the domain `lac.inf.puc-rio.br` and that is a base context type: i.e. inherites from the base type `Context`.

---

[2] The user that models a new context.

```xml
<?xml version="1.0"?>
<context name="DeviceContext"
          domain="lac.inf.puc-rio.br"
          package="moca.context"
          base="Context">
    <entity name="DeviceMacAddress"
                   type="xs:string" kind="entity">
        Device's MAC address
    </entity>
    <attribute name="CpuUsage"
                   type="xs:int" static="no">
        Percentual of CPU usage
    </attribute>
    <attribute name="FreeMemory"
                   type="xs:int" static="no">
        Available memory in kb
    </attribute>
    <attribute name="BatteryPower"
                   type="xs:int" static="no">
        Percentual of the full power available on
        the battery
    </attribute>
    <attribute name="IpAddress"
                   type="xs:string" static="no">
        IP Address
    </attribute>
    <attribute name="IpMask"
                   type="xs:string" static="no">
        IP Mask
    </attribute>
</context>
```

6.6 Programming Model

The snippet below exemplifies the creation of an interest for the type Device
Context for the condition Battery <70%.

```
ContextInterest appInterest =
               DeviceContext.newInterest();
appInterest.id("AA:0A:12:...").where(
               DeviceContext.Attr.BATTERY.lt(70).
appInterest.register(interestListener);
```

The deployment of `DeviceContext`'s DCMML file generates a library (a jar file) that contains the class `DeviceContext`. Any interest for `DeviceContext` and for any of its subtypes is constructed through the object returned from `newInterest()` invocation. The method `id(<entity-id>)` indicates the entity parameter of the interest and `where` indicates the constraints of the interest. Notice that each attribute of the type contains a corresponding attribute in the generated class that allows the construction of the constraint: for the attribute `Battery`, the Context Tool generated a static attribute `Attr.BATTERY` that must be used to include the aforementioned attribute in a constraint. It restricts an application to describe an invalid constraint and the middleware does not need to revalidate a constraint at runtime. At the last line of the snippet, the application registers the interest and informs the listener to be invoked at any notification.

References

1. Guttman, E., Perkins, C., Veizades, J., Day, M.: Service Location Protocol, Version 2. Technical Report IETF RFC 2608, (1999)
2. Pallickara, S., Fox, G.: Naradabrokering: a distributed middleware framework and architecture for enabling durable peer-to-peer grids. In: Middleware '03: Proceedings of the ACM/IFIP/USENIX 2003 International Conference on Middleware, pp. 41–61. Springer-Verlag, New York (2003)

Chapter 7
Implementation and Evaluation

Abstract The feasibility of the context domains approach for context management is demonstrated through an implementation of a distributed middleware. Test results have shown that the implementation's performance is appropriate to the target scenario. The event engine of the middleware is based on a distributed event-based system called Naradabrokering. In particular, the middleware adopts Naradabrokering's XML engine. Context information is represented as XML events, which the engine matches with context interests described in XPath expressions. This middleware allows the development of context-aware applications for mobile devices, and runs in two platforms: Android and Java J2ME CDC 1.1.

Keywords Context management · Implementation · Middleware · Distributed architectures

7.1 Introduction

The goal of this chapter is to describe details of the middleware implementation and to validate the proposed approach presented in previous chapters. This chapter is organized as follows. Section 7.2 presents the implementation of the middleware in terms of cNode and CMN. Section 7.3 presents the testing environment adopted to evaluate the middleware. The tests described in Sect. 7.4 aim at evaluating how the proposed architecture supports a feasible scenario. The tests evaluate how the middleware scales with interest wideness, and the impact of the number of clients and evolution in the middleware performance.

7.2 Implementation

The implementation of the middleware is composed of two main components: the cNode, which runs in portable devices, and the CMN, that is a middleware instance that runs in each host responsible for a particular context domain. The context-aware

R. C. A. da Rocha and M. Endler, *Context Management for Distributed and Dynamic*   73
Context-Aware Computing, SpringerBriefs in Computer Science,
DOI: 10.1007/978-1-4471-4020-7_7, © The Author(s) 2012

ecosystem is composed of a network of CMN, which are responsible for managing cNode (i.e. client devices) in a domain.

In mobile devices, the prototype is based on the Android platform[1], whereas Java is the development plataform for the middleware services in wired networks.

7.2.1 Client Node

The cNode is an Android service shared among applications that runs in a device. cNode is implemented in a service called CMS, which runs in a different process of context consumers and providers. cNode implements the following AIDL[2] interface:

```
interface ICMS {
    void publish(IContext context);
    void register(IContextInterest interest);
    void addListener(IContextInterest interest,
                     IInterestListener listener);
    void unregister(IContextInterest interest);
}
```

As any Android service, the access to the CMS uses interprocess communication to implement the communication between the service and any consumer or provider. Figure 7.1 shows the interaction of this service and context providers and consumers, through the architectural layers of Android OS.

In an Android service, parameter passing in interprocess communication is implemented through serialization/deserialization of objects. Android remote objects allow parameters as Java/Dalvik basic types, *parcelable* objects or remote objects. In the latter case, an object is not serialized and an invocation of its methods corresponds to another remote method invocation. A parcelable object is the Android's implementation of serializable objects with two differences: they must have a parcelable interface (in a corresponding AIDL) at development time, and serialization/deserialization must be explicitly programmed by the developer. Since each context type stub is developed and deployed latter than the cNode, its interface cannot be predicted and cannot be used in the interface of the CMS service. For this reason, the middleware also implements the context type and interest as remote objects, based on the interfaces IContext and IContextInterest, below.

```
interface IContext {
    String getId();
    String getDomain();
    long getTimestamp();
    boolean isLocal();
```

---

[1] The first implementation was based on Android 0.9.

[2] Android IDL language

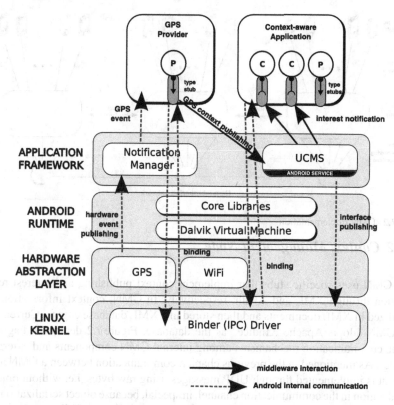

Fig. 7.1 Interaction among consumers, providers and the CMS service in the Android implementation

```
    String getPublisherExpressionImpl();
}

interface IContextInterest {
    void addListener(IInterestListener listener);
    String getInterestImpl();
    void register();
    void unregister();
}
```

The methods getPublisherExpressionImpl() and getInterest
Impl() from interfaces IContext and IContextInterest, respectively,
return the query for publishing and consuming context. These queries are
environment-specific: an Android stub for a cNode uses SQL queries targeting the
Android's SQLLite internal database, where context information is stored. A stub
for a CMN uses XPath, as described in the next section.

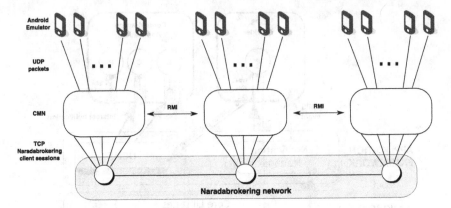

Fig. 7.2 CMN implementation

7.2.2 Context Management Node

The CMN uses specific stubs that implement context publishing and interest registration through XML and XPath, respectively. In CMN, context information is serialized in XML documents and then stored in a XML database engine. Currently, the CMN adopts Apache XIndice[3] as the database. Figure 7.2 depicts a diagram of the communication mechanisms among internal CMN components and external entities. As mentioned in the previous chapter, communication between a CMN and a client is implemented through UDP messages using raw bytes, i.e. without object serialization in the communication channel, in special, because object serialization of Dalvik VM is incompatible with serialization of Java VM[4]. The CMN runs inside a EJB container and uses RMI for communication among CMN instances, in different domains.

Each client proxy corresponds to a unique session of communication to Naradabrokering, with a respective Naradabrokering *client id*, as shown in Fig. 7.2. Each consumer and provider proxy is implemented as a respective Naradabrokering consumer and provider, built in the same client session. When a client device migrates to another domain, CMN closes the respective Naradabrokering session and eventually starts another session with the Naradabrokering instance of the new CMN.

7.3 Testing Scenario

The testing scenario is composed of instances of CMN running in a same local network. To simulate several domains in a same local network, the discovery service was disabled. Client devices were simulated as processes in a same machine, statically configured with a specific domain.

---

[3] http://xml.apache.org/xindice/

[4] At least, until version 0.9 of Android SDK, on which this implementation prototype is based on.

Functional tests used the Android emulator as a client device, which is based on the QEMU, an open source processor emulator. The testing script was developed to run with Apache's JMeter[5]. The testing environment is composed of Pentium 4 and two Core 2 Duo machines, each one with 1Gb in memory, connected through a 100Mbps local network.

7.4 Scalability Tests

This section analyses the performance of the middleware based on the results of scalability tests. These tests are organized in two categories:

- Tests of performance of the middleware in stress conditions, which involves connection with a large number of clients in a CMN.
- Effect of the mobility in the service, in terms of the cost of migrating proxies between CMNs.

7.4.1 Service Performance

7.4.1.1 Management of Proxies in a CMN

Management of proxies in a CMN is one of the most important tasks of the middleware, since interest registration and matching is delegated to the event service (Naradabrokering). It interferes directly in the scalability with clients of the middleware, since each client has a correspondent proxy in a CMN. A proxy may be composed of several consumer and provider proxies. The impact in mobility is analysed in Sect. 7.4.2.

As a preparation step for this test, another test showed that Naradabrokering cannot deal with more than 200 concurrent clients. When managing more than 200 clients, the Naradabrokering protocol for client initialization performs with long delays that cause message timeout and the consequent disconnection of clients. For this reason, all of the following tests use this limit number of clients in a CMN.

The test evaluated the delay of creation of client, consumer and provider proxies, as depicted in Figs. 7.3, 7.4a and b, respectively. Both consumers and providers depend on a previous existing client proxy. Figure 7.3 shows a linear behavior for creation of proxies in a CMN. Figures 7.4a and b shows that the delay of creating proxies for consumers and providers do not have a significant impact, considering that this delay also includes remote calls to a CMN. In fact, the delay for creation of client proxies shown in Fig. 7.3 is more significant then the aforementioned delays. For example, the delay for creating 1000 consumer or provider proxies is lesser then

---

[5] http://jakarta.apache.org/jmeter

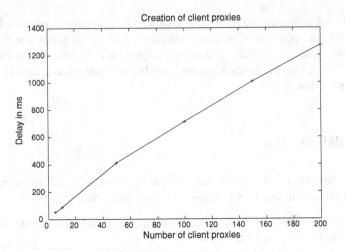

Fig. 7.3 Delay of client proxy creation

900 ms, whereas this delay is sufficient for creating less then 140 client proxies. Such difference is due to the fact that creation of a consumer proxy requires a creation of a new connection between a CMN and the Naradabrokering, whereas the creation of a consumer and a provider proxy does not produce any new Naradabrokering connections.

7.4.1.2 Access to Context Maintained in Distributed Domains

This test evaluates the performance of a CMN in serving context consumers, in terms of the delay of receiving notifications of interest match. This evaluation is composed of two parts: a test of dissemination using a single CMN and using a small network of CMNs.

A network of CMNs has a corresponding network of Naradabrokering nodes. A network of Naradabrokering nodes is based on a hierarchical construction of node relationships. In a Naradabrokering network, each node has an address composed of four 5-bit numbers, for example, 23.20.31.14. Each part of the address has a limit of 32. A Naradabrokering network is a hierarchical network of nodes, aggregated in clusters according to node's addresses. The lower-level node is called unit. A network of 32 nodes comprehends a cluster, which is controlled by one of its nodes called cluster controller. A network of 32 clusters is controlled by a super-cluster controller, whereas a network of 32 super-clusters is controlled by a super-cluster controller, as illustrated by Fig. 7.5. The nodes 23.20.31.14 and 23.20.31.21 are part of a same network that is controlled by the cluster controller that has the same cluster prefix 23.20.31.

A node in clusters, super-clusters or super-super-clusters controller is responsible for disseminating events on the network it controls.

Fig. 7.4 Delay for creation of provider and consumer proxies

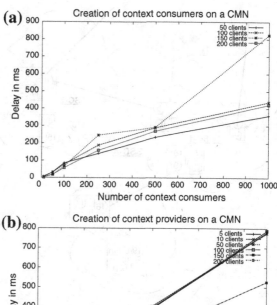

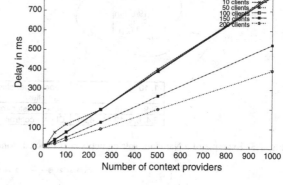

The network of nodes in a cluster follows no previously defined organization. During the deployment of the nodes, the user chooses the more appropriate organization of nodes and selects special nodes (or dedicated machines without nodes) to act as brokers, i.e. gateways among nodes and clusters, responsible for event dissemination. To facilitate the test, the testing scenario adopted a network configuration where each node in a cluster has a direct connection to the broker, and there is only one broker for a cluster, as shown in Fig. 7.6. In this organization, the max height of the hierarchy tree is four, and thus, the max distance among two nodes in the network is seven Naradabrokering connections.

This test used eight hosts to simulate a larger distance among nodes. In order to increase the load in each node, each CMN will serve 100 clients, from 50 to 1000 consumers. Another parameter is the complexity if the interest expression. To simulate this complexity, the test used a simple context type with string attributes. Each attribute of the context type will participate in the expression. The tests used context types with number of attributes changing from 1 to 20, but no relevant difference was found. Figure 7.7 shows the result of the tests for a type with 20 attributes and all of them introduced in the constraint of the context interest.

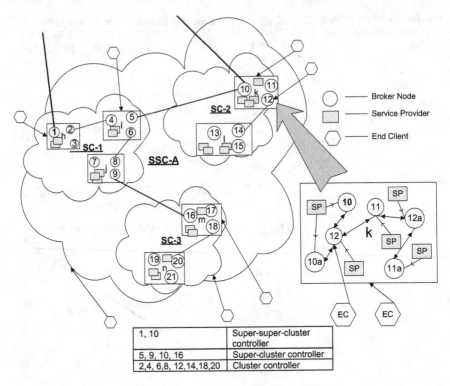

1, 10	Super-super-cluster controller
5, 9, 10, 16	Super-cluster controller
2,4, 6,8, 12,14,18,20	Cluster controller

Fig. 7.5 Example of a Naradabrokering network (extracted from [4])

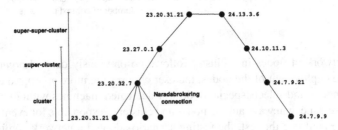

Fig. 7.6 Max distance between two Naradabrokering nodes

7.4.2 Mobility Impact

This test evaluates the impact of mobility in the middleware performance, in terms of the overhead of moving client proxies from one CMN to another CMN. The test moves constantly proxies between CMNs in a scenario with no providers to avoid the interference of context dissemination in proxy migration. A transference of a proxy comprehends the restart of a Naradabrokering session, the serialization/deserialization of the client proxy, and update in the Entity Home where the proxy has interests. The test ignores the delay introduced by the last task. Figure 7.8

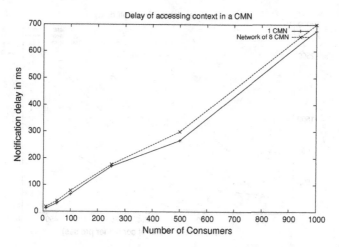

Fig. 7.7 Delay of accessing context in a CMN

shows the results of the tests with 10, 50 and 100 concurrent clients. Each of these tests used the proxy size (number of consumers) assuming the values of 50, 100, 250 and 500. The results show an exponential grow of the hand-off delay. The results confirm a prediction during the development of the middleware: Naradabrokering does not offer suitable APIs to implement a hand-off. There is no primitive to interrupt a connection with a broker, serialize all Naradabrokering consumers and providers and restart the connection with another Naradabrokering service. As result, the implementation of the hand-off became inefficient by requiring the removal and construction of all consumers and providers in the new Naradabrokering context. However, in the practice, client tends to have a smaller number of proxies than the numbers used in the test. For example, a proxy with size of 50 consumers implies in a single device with 50 context interests.

7.5 Limitations

In spite of its several benefits, the proposed middleware for context management has some intrinsec limitations, discussed in the following sections.

7.5.1 Basic Mechanism for Context-Based Adaptation

The mechanism of interest registration and notification is a basic mechanism for context-based adaptation. However, complex context-aware applications demand higher-level abstractions for adaptation, such as adaptation *profiles* (e.g., as adopted

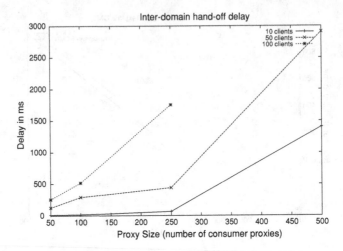

Fig. 7.8 Hand-off processing delay

in MobiPADS [2] and CARISMA [1]) and PACE's *preferences* [3]. These abstractions can be implemented at the basis of interest registrations and notifications. For example, an adaptation profile is essentially an abstraction of a set of pre-defined interests. In a distributed scenario, however, the implementation of a context management middleware that supports such high-level abstractions is a challenging task, because they cannot be easily shared through the concept of context domains and the usage of some of them (e.g., *preferences*) is restricted to a specific user scope. Hence, the proposed middleware aims at providing just a basic mechanism for supporting context-aware applications in distributed environments. This work suggests that higher-level abstraction should be supported at higher layers of context management middleware.

7.5.2 Chain of Providers and Consumers Causes Delays of Context Reasoning

The efficiency of the distributed context manangement is based on the data-oriented modeling approach (Sect. 4.2). As a result, the inference of new context information must be based on the implementation of inference agents, which act as consumers of a context and providers of the inferred context. The implementation of complex context reasoning, produced by a sequence of inferences, may require the introduction of a chain of inference agents (pairs of consumer-providers). This chain cases delay in interest notification, which may hinder fast triggering of context-based adaptations.

7.5.3 Context Domains Strongly Based on Network Domain

The proposed implementation of context domains is strictly based on network domains. This approach eases the implementation of domain discovery, which in the proposed middleware is based on SLP. However, in some scenarios, a context domain would be more appropriately mapped to a physical area, instead of a network domain. For example, in the usage scenario of Chap. 5, to switch to the domain rio.downtown.mnba, the user needs to connect to MNBA's local network. Thus, if the user carries a device (e.g. a mobile phone) that has no WiFi connectivity, then he will not be able to switch to the more specific domain, even if the application scenario requires such location-specific context access.

7.5.4 Interoperability Among Domains Enforced by the Adoption of Standards

The distributed approach for context management is also strongly based on the assumption that the context models of each domain promotes concept sharing and extension in subdomains.

The requirements discussed in Sect 2.4 cannot be achieved if the models of different domains are not based on concepts of a common superdomain. Moreover, this book does not propose any methodology to promote such appropriate context modeling or to evaluate the adequacy of a distributed model.

References

1. Capra, L., Emmerich, W., Mascolo, C.: CARISMA: context-aware reflective middleware system for mobile applications. IEEE Trans. Softw. Eng. **29**(10), 929–945 (2003). doi:10.1109/TSE. 2003.1237173
2. Chan, A.T.S., Chuang, S.N.: MobiPADS: a reflective middleware for context-aware mobile computing. IEEE Trans. Softw. Eng. **29**(12), 1072–1085 (2003).
3. Henricksen, K., Indulska, J.: Developing context-aware pervasive computing applications: Models and approach. Pervasive and Mobile Computing **2**(1), 37–64 (2006). doi:10.1016/j. pmcj.2005.07.003
4. Pallikara, S., Fox, G.: Naradabrokering: a distributed middleware framework and architecture for enabling durable peer-to-peer grids. Middleware '03: Proceedings of the ACM/IFIP/USENIX 2003 International Conference on Middleware, pp. 41–61. Springer-Verlag New York, Inc., New York (2003)

Chapter 8
Conclusions

Abstract Context management based on context domains is an approach for supporting interests of variable wideness, which is a fundamental requirement to context-aware computing in distributed and dynamic environments. This work explored this concept and presented three additional contributions: a primitive to describe context interests of variable wideness, the design and implementation of a middleware that support context domains, and a categorization of architectures for supporting distributed context-aware computing.

Keywords Distributed context management · Context-aware computing · Middleware · Context evolution

8.1 Introduction

Middleware systems for dynamic context-aware ecosystems have several implementation challenges. As the ecosystem grows in size, diversity of sensors and devices, and complexity, middleware systems have to absorb the environment's evolution and to keep the consistency of the application's interests. In such a scenario, an ecosystem should be a composition of interrelated environments for context-aware computing, instead of a set of isolated environments.

Most of current middleware systems make restrictive assumptions about enabling distributed context-aware computing such as the adoption of a single context model and that context interests must be statically linked to CMSs. These assumptions restrict the description of context interests to ecosystems with predictable and well-known structure, behavior and distribution. Hence, these middleware systems may cause disruptions or inconsistencies in applications that have cross-environment interests. Current federation-based systems hinder scalability and manageability, since they also adopt a unified context model for a whole ecosystem.

R. C. A. da Rocha and M. Endler, *Context Management for Distributed and Dynamic Context-Aware Computing*, SpringerBriefs in Computer Science, DOI: 10.1007/978-1-4471-4020-7_8, © The Author(s) 2012

This book advocates that dynamic context-aware ecosystems require a new class of context interests, called *context interests of variable wideness*. This class of context interests is particularly difficult to implement in current middleware systems, because it requires an interest delivery layer that dynamically discovers which CMSs and context types satisfies each interest. Chapter 5 described a usage scenario that demonstrates how such interests enable the development of simpler and generic applications, in terms of interaction with a diversity of context providers.

This book described an architecture to support context interests of variable wideness, in which an ecosystem is a set of hierarchically and dynamically composed context domains. Each context domain may have particular context providers and models, thus enabling heterogeneous modeling. The architecture supports contextual interoperability through the establishment of subtyping relationships among models of different domains. A context interest can span a variable set of CMS/domains and types, according to the need of the context consumer. The feasibility of this approach is based on two fundamental assumptions. Firstly, the approach assumes that management of context instances and context models are loosely-coupled, i.e. the context modeling approach does not support the description of rules to infer new context instances. Instead, only context providers can publish new instances. In addition, the idea of Entity Home provides an efficient mechanism to dynamically discover which domains contain context for a given entity. Chapter 6 described the implementation of a middleware that supports context domains.

According to the classification proposed in Chap. 3, a middleware based on context domains is a distributed middleware system. However, differently from other approaches, the CMS discovery is highly dynamic and distributed, whereas state-of-the-art work (e.g. PACE) adopts a centralized registry of CMSs.

One of the fundamental characteristics of a context-aware ecosystem is the adoption of heterogeneous context models. Indeed, the support of model heterogeneity enables each CMS to manage types that are relevant to an environment or administration domain. Federation-based and bridging-based approaches adequately deal with interoperability issues of heterogeneous CMS (i.e. heterogeneous primitives). However, their mechanisms for model management are clearly not scalable, since they map models of each CMS to a unified model.

The context domain approach for context management aims at providing a basic lower-level layer for context management. In this sense, more complex adaptation abstractions, such as *preferences* of PACE middleware, and context modeling constructions should be provided on top of the proposed middleware. For this reason, this book adopted a lower-level concept of context information, based on the concept originally proposed in ContextToolkit. Currently, research in context-aware computing adopts a more comprehensive concept of context information, defining context as a part of a process, instead of just a state [2]. However, for lower-level context management, the definition adopted in this book is appropriate.

In order to implement the basic tasks of a CMS, middleware systems usually adopt general-purpose asynchronous event-based systems. The proposed middleware adopted Naradabrokering as the basic asynchronous communication mechanism. The experience of designing middleware for dynamic ecosystems has shown that such general purpose systems lack three important characteristics. Firstly, they do not support an *extensible, distributed, and flexible data model* that enables the mapping of context models through distributed domains. Moreover, their *subscription paradigms* do not enable the implementation of interests that comprehend event providers in a dynamic set of nodes in distributed event system. However, there is also a trade-off between expressiveness and the scalability of a general-purpose distributed event-based system [1]. Finally, they usually do not provide a *lightweight communication protocol* to use with resource-constrained portable devices.

In face of such limitation, the proposed middleware used a flexible event type (XML), to enable the mapping of context types and interests in the scope of the Naradabrokeringsystem. A clear consequence of this design decision is the performance degradation of interest (i.e. event) matching. Therefore, middleware for dynamic context-aware ecosystems calls for an event-based system that enables object-oriented events, distributed object type models, and dynamic deployment of nodes. There is not a distributed event-based system that satisfies such requirements.

8.2 Summary of Contributions

The work presented in this book presents four main contributions:

Concept of Context Domains

Context domains are a novel architecture for organizing distributed context-aware systems in an integrated and dynamic ecosystem. Differently from other approaches, context domains enable the idea of scope in context-aware computing, both in terms of promoting the adequacy of environment to the particularities of an administrative domain, as well, to enable applications to restrict the domains where their context interests will be applied.

Primitive for Describing Context Interests of Variable Wideness

This work advocates that applications demand for primitives to describe consistent and comprehensive context interests, despite the dynamic and distributed characteristics of a context-aware ecosystem. The proposed primitive enables applications to describe context interests of variable wideness, which in turn describes an interest comprising open, closed or relative domains of context management systems, and more specific or abstract context types. The proposed primitive allows the development of applications that are both more generic and, at the same time, simpler.

Design of a Middleware Based on Context Domains

In order to demonstrate the feasibility of the proposed approach, this book described the design and implementation of a distributed middleware based on the concept of context domains. The middleware adopts a dual mode of context management that integrates consumers and providers that are either of a same device or distributed in different domains. The feasibility of the middleware execution on portable devices was verified through tests in an emulated Android-based device.

Categorization of Architectures for Supporting Distributed Context-Aware Computing

This book also presents an original classification of architectures for distributed context-aware computing. According to this classification, distributed middleware adopts one of the following approaches for context management: distributed middleware systems, peer-to-peer approaches, federation-based approaches or bridging approaches. The proposed classification is useful to understand the trade-offs and limitations of each approach.

8.3 Future Research

This work provides fundamental concepts and mechanisms to deal with dynamic context-aware ecosystems. Future research can explore these basic mechanisms to promote the use of the middleware in more realistic scenarios, and to promote efficiency, security and manageability. This section describes some of future research efforts that can be developed as a direct extension of this work.

8.3.1 Context Domains Based on Physical Location

In the proposed architecture, the implementation of context domains is strictly based on network domains, i.e. a change of network topology implies in a domain change. As discussed in Sect. 7.5.3, this approach for defining context domains introduces limitations for the usage of the middleware in real scenarios. A direct extension of this work is to relax the assumptions described in Sect. 4.3, and provide means to describe context domains based on physical location of devices and users.

8.3.2 Extension of Constraint Operation in a Context Interest

The context tool maps an interest constraint to an expression based on SQL or XPath operators, depending if the stub is used in a cNode or a CMN . Hence, the complexity of a constraint is bounded by the operators of these query languages. Although they provide a comprehensive set of operators for basic language types (e.g. integer, string), a context type may demand the description of specific operators. For example, a location type could provide operations such as distance, proximity and containment of a location in an area. Such type-specific operators increase code readability and decrease the chance of misinterpretation of type semantics. As a future work, an extension of the context modeling approach could enable the description of context-specific operators through the inclusion of the code of an operator in a DCMML file of a type.

8.3.3 Composition of Notifications Based on Context Meta-Attributes

Another aspect to explore in a future work is the introduction of meta-attributes in the modeling of a context, to enable consumers to indicate additional restrictions to an interest based on properties of the provider or the context publication. Consider that several providers publish a same abstract context for a given entity, causing thus several notifications to a consumer. A consumer may indicate in the interest expression the properties of the more appropriate notification to the consumer needs. For example, the consumer may indicate a preference for notifications from the provider of the most precise data or even with a minimum precision. In this example, *precision* is a property of the provider, which must be previously indicated to the middleware to be checked against consumer's interests. Research in context-aware computing calls quality of context the usage of these meta-attributes to define preferences or requirements of a consumer.

8.3.4 Implementation Policies for Optimized Context Access

The context meta-information, obtained from the context model, enables the middleware to choose the most suitable mechanisms to handle certain context information. For example, consider a context attribute declared as static, i.e. an attribute that has a constant value (e.g. the OS type/version running at a device). When deploying this context, the context management infrastructure is configured so as to disseminate and update this attribute only at the first time when an application requests the context. The context tool uses these meta-information to implement optimized stubs.

8.3.5 Security Mechanisms for Inter-Domain Context Management

The proposed middleware requires the introduction of the following security mechanisms:

- Authentication and validation of providers that publish context for a given entity. This authentication can avoid malicious provides to disseminate false context information.
- Authentication of consumers and clients (device).
- Validation of domains, to guarantee that the interaction among domains and the algorithm for context dissemination (described Sect. 6.3.3) performs correctly. Otherwise, a malicious or fake CMN could manipulate messages to the Entity Home to deceive mechanism for controlling context access (e.g. for privacy concerns).

Moreover, support for privacy is an important requirement for context-aware architectures, which is beyond the focus of this book. However, the usage of a Entity Home provides an interesting approach for control privacy of context access, since it is a central point of access for a given entity's context. A user can control the dissemination context for some consumers through the Entity Home . Hesselman [3] proposed a similar mechanism for privacy control based on the idea of a home node, responsible for controlling all context information of a given user.

8.3.6 Enhanced Model of Interaction Among Providers, Consumers and CMS

The proposed middleware adopts a simple model of interaction among providers, consumers and the CMS. In this model, providers are always active elements that publish context constantly, independently of existing consumers. On one hand, the context information is more accurate, in terms of freshness, if a provider publishes at a higher rate. On the other hand, constant publications increase the number of messages sent through a network, even if there is no consumer for the aforementioned information. For some providers, a publication is a costly operation, in terms of battery usage (e.g. WiFi scanner) and messages sent through the network.

Hence, in a future research, the middleware could introduce an additional model of interaction, enabling providers to publish on demand, i.e. when there is a corresponding consumer. This model demands a previous registration by each provider of which entity it may publish context, in order to include the provider in the Entity Home table and, thus, enabling its discovery.

References

1. Carzaniga, A., Rosenblum, D.S., Wolf, A.L.: Achieving scalability and expressiveness in an internet-scale event notification service. In: Proceedings of the nineteenth annual ACM symposium on principles of distributed computing, pp. 219–227, Portland (2000)
2. Coutaz, J., Crowley, J.L., Dobson, S., Garlan, D.: Context is key. Commun. ACM **48**(3), 49–53 (2005). doi:10.1145/1047671.1047703
3. Hesselman, C., Eertink, H., Wibbels, M.: Privacy-aware context discovery for next generation mobile services. In: Proceedings of the 2007 international symposium on applications and the internet workshops (SAINTW'07), pp. 3–6 (2007). doi:10.1109/SAINT-W.2007.87, IEEE Computer Seciety, Washington, DC